# Advance

D0596135

"*Bart is engaging, inspiring and full of energy. I have enjoyed watching his continued success. Bart is living proof that if you 'Dig Your Well Before You're Thirsty,' you can strike gold.*"

—HARVEY MACKAY, AUTHOR OF THE BESTSELLING
*SWIM WITH THE SHARKS WITHOUT BEING EATEN ALIVE*

"*I love everything about BusinessOutside—Bart is an inspiration and proof that living an intentional life can lead to a healthier and happier life.*"

—DR. JOHN AGWUNOBI, MD, CHAIRMAN AND CEO OF HERBALIFE NUTRITION AND FORMER
PRESIDENT OF HEALTH & WELLNESS AT WALMART

"*BusinessOutside provides teams with a mental, emotional, and physical reset. The approach Bart Foster has built and describes is something all business leaders can benefit from by redefining how our relationships, work, and personal lives can be better integrated.*"

—JOHN RYAN, CEO OF UNITEDHEALTHCARE GROUP

"*BusinessOutside provides a path to getting outside of your comfort zone, away from the screen, in the open air, freeing the brain and soul to make more meaningful connections with others.*"

—CARLA PINEYRO SUBLETT, CHIEF MARKETING OFFICER AT IBM

"With BusinessOutside, Bart Foster delivers a message that is inspirational, aspirational, and important. It's time to start busting through some walls!"

—FLORENCE WILLIAMS, AUTHOR OF *THE NATURE FIX: WHY NATURE MAKES US HAPPIER, HEALTHIER, AND MORE CREATIVE*

"I have seen firsthand how Bart uses BusinessOutside to lead teams to think differently—outside their comfort zone, outside normal business practices, and outside in nature."

—ANDY PAWSON, PRESIDENT AND GM AT ALCON

"Bart is one of the most engaging and energetic people I've ever met—an inspiration for living an intentional life that amplifies health and happiness. BusinessOutside is the perfect antidote to our new pandemic life and will dramatically grow in importance as people seek a new normal."

—DAVID CUMMINGS, CEO OF ATLANTA VENTURES

"A vivid exemplar on the benefits of intentional living and working outside the box."

—READE FAHS, CEO OF NATIONAL VISION

# BUSINESS OUTSIDE

## Discover Your Path Forward

BART FOSTER

**LIONCREST**
PUBLISHING

Copyright © 2022 Bart Foster

*All rights reserved.*

**BusinessOutside**

*Discover Your Path Forward*

ISBN   978-1-5445-3074-1  Hardcover
          978-1-5445-3075-8  Paperback
          978-1-5445-3076-5  Ebook

*To Aly, AK, and Owen,*

*who support my crazy adventures,*

*give me the space to find my own path,*

*and always believe in me to*

*Make it Happen!*

# Contents

# Introduction

IN JANUARY 2021, I WENT FOR A HIKE ON THE MOUNTAIN BEHIND my house in Boulder, Colorado. It was an activity I returned to many times because of the way it would rejuvenate and re-energize me physically, mentally, and emotionally. On the mountain, new ideas were easy to come by. Creative inspiration didn't feel so far off. I could see more clearly and breathe more deeply. Perhaps most importantly, being outside simply made me happier.

On this particular hike up the mountain, a simple thought hit me: *I want everyone to operate in this zone.* And in that moment, the idea for BusinessOutside® was born.

Part of my mission now is to motivate people to get outside—*literally and figuratively*. To spend time outside in the great outdoors, and to operate outside outdated corporate norms.

Too many of us are stuck "inside"—inside our video calls, inside our corporate hierarchy, inside our self-imposed limitations about what's possible, and inside unrealized potential. BusinessOutside is an antidote to the "inside" culture that is permeating corporations around the world. It's an antidote for both executives and employees who need genuine connections and the space to bring their authentic selves so they can feel empowered and energized.

Since 2020, I have been testing my BusinessOutside principles with executives and teams across North America, including Fortune 500 companies. I knew it would be successful, but the response has blown me away. We are creating a movement. I can feel it.

Following a science-inspired philosophy, we teach BusinessOutside principles to help people feel psychologically restored. In our retreats, we invite participants to tap into their true, authentic selves in a natural setting. People leave healthier, more creative, inspired, and renewed by experiencing genuine connections. By using BusinessOutside methods, business leaders can create organizational cultures that nurture and empower their people, helping them discover their path forward.

While BusinessOutside principles and methods are applicable to all at any time, they are critical in our post-pandemic world. The future of work will be hybrid, and remote workforces will crave flexibility, but still need the connection that can only come through in-person interactions. The return of the corporate retreat is coming, but it won't be like the boondoggles of the past. It will be a place to reenergize and return to alignment in every way.

In this book, I outline many of the principles and methods we teach on our retreats. These are the same principles and methods I use with my personal clients. I have seen their impact across countless teams and businesses. This book is for executive leaders, entrepreneurs, and business owners. I've written it as a guidebook to give you the direction you need to navigate how to think differently and lead effectively.

It's time to rethink how we do business. And that starts by tapping into your unique skills, passions, and creativity, so that you can then empower your team to do the same. It starts by recognizing there's no "professional" you and "personal" you. There's just you.

The problem is that many of us continue on paths we don't truly want to walk, so we constantly feel torn. We often do this without conscious thought. In the end, we are no longer leading our own lives; instead, life is happening *to* us. I remember when I first realized that I needed to shake things up. I was living a comfortable life, but everything was happening *to me*. When I was finally honest with myself, I saw that my life was not actually built *by* me. I needed to step back and figure out what I truly wanted, what made me happy. Then I needed to put a plan in place to make it happen.

In this book, I will challenge you to step back and be honest with yourself so that you, too, can blaze a new trail—the one you want to be on. By going on this journey, you will discover your path forward. You will learn to embrace a new philosophy as you make your way into nature and beyond self-imposed comfort zones.

In each chapter, you'll be equipped with a new tool to take with you on the journey. You will learn how to create a personal values statement. You will learn to identify and harness your Zone of Genius, which will provide clarity about your next steps in life and work. As you shift to spending the majority of your time in your Zone of Genius, you will be happier and healthier, and you will inevitably elevate everyone around you. You will also learn how to be assertive and proactive about your career, expand your circle of comfort, pinpoint what is holding you back, identify decision-making accelerants, and determine the people, books, and resources that will support you in your growth. If you feel you are lost in the wilderness, stuck, unhappy, unfulfilled, or dissatisfied, my hope is that this book will help you realize what's possible and inspire you to take action. It is intended to help you shift your mindset, reorient your life, and carve a path that will ultimately make you happier. Happier individuals lead to better, more productive companies. In the end, everyone wins.

Now is the time to challenge the status quo, push boundaries, find creative ways to conduct business, and get yourself and your team outside.

Now is the time to create a life you love. It's time to do BusinessOutside.

# CHAPTER ONE

# BusinessOutside

> *"Thousands of tired, nerve-shaken, over-civilized people are beginning to find out that going to the mountains is going home; that wildness is a necessity."*
>
> —JOHN MUIR

FIFTY-FIVE PEOPLE SHOWED UP AT 5:00 A.M. ON A WEDNESDAY morning to hike the Boulder Skyline Traverse. I couldn't believe it. This twenty-mile hike, with 6,000 feet of elevation gain, isn't for beginners. The group had started modestly enough, with a few friends who were going to hike every major peak in the mountain range in Boulder, Colorado. Within three weeks, it had evolved into a curated group of entrepreneurs and business owners who all had one thing in common: a growth mindset.

I shouldn't have been surprised; this was one of the reasons my family and I had moved to Boulder in the first place: the opportunity to surround ourselves with people who prioritized getting outside.

And when I formed this group, I had set the intention that it be a place for deep connection. Still, seeing my dreams come to fruition felt unreal. Here I was, doing what I had set out to do—to create a whole new life.

Three years before, in 2014, I found myself at a crossroads. After I left SoloHealth, a technology company I had founded seven years earlier, I took time off to travel with my family and discover my identity without the CEO title. I reconnected with friends and family I hadn't seen in years, and engaged in meaningful discussions. My wife, Aly, and I spent countless hours reflecting on what was most important to us. It didn't take long for us to acknowledge that our lives had become too routine. We needed to shake things up.

I thought back to the several cross-country moves in my life—one from Illinois to California when I was eight years old and a second from California to Florida when I was fourteen. After college I moved from Florida, to Texas, to Michigan, with Kellogg's, then to Atlanta where I worked with the eye care division of Novartis. With each move, there were dramatic environmental and cultural changes that shaped who I became. I learned the value of getting out of my comfort zone at an early age, which expanded my capacity to be adaptable in all areas.

As these thoughts ran through my mind, I reached out to friends who I knew could add perspective to our situation. Jim Sharpe, fellow member of Young Presidents' Organization (YPO) and respected business school professor, told me about the "zip code strategy": pick where you want to live first, and then figure it out from there. I had never heard of this concept, but it made sense to me. Why not live in a place that reflects your ideal lifestyle?

Soon enough, Aly and I were Googling all the best places to do the things most important to us:

- Best places to raise a family
- Best cities to walk
- Healthiest cities
- Best cities for entrepreneurs
- Best places for outdoor adventure

It turned out that Boulder, Colorado, was at the top of nearly every list. So off we went to see why people seemed to love this place so much.

Within hours of walking around the city, breathing the crisp, clean air, marveling at the majestic mountains, and talking to the kinds of people we could easily imagine having as neighbors, we knew it was the place for us. Over the next three weeks, we sold more than half our material possessions, packed the rest into our car, and took the long, scenic drive from Atlanta, Georgia, into the great unknown.

## MY FIRST OUTDOOR MEETING

Soon after we arrived in Boulder, I knew I needed to begin meeting people and expanding my network, perhaps looking for a business to buy or invest in. I reached out to a small list of people and asked them to have coffee or lunch. That was, after all, the appropriate course of action, or so I thought.

One of the first people I reached out to was Elizabeth Kraus, a local venture capitalist and business executive. When Elizabeth suggested we meet at the trailhead and go for a "hiking meeting," I was taken aback. It felt so strange and unusual. *But why not?* I thought. Hadn't I moved for the outdoor lifestyle? Hadn't I wanted to go outside my comfort zone again? I didn't even know what to wear, but I put on whatever seemed right and showed up. As they say, the rest is history. That day completely changed my perspective and my path in life.

As it turned out, I absolutely loved meeting outdoors. On that hike, I realized for the first time that I didn't have to be behind a desk to conduct business. *Who knew?* Sure enough, I was hooked.

I started by taking phone calls outside. This evolved to one-on-one, and group coaching meetings outdoors. On the trail, I could build more authentic relationships and have deeper conversations. "Hiking meetings" became my default. And three years later, I found myself lacing up my trail shoes on a Wednesday with fifty-five people who, like me, were looking for worthwhile and purposeful interactions.

## WHY ARE WE IN A CUBE?

Humans have been on earth for two million years and spent most of their time outside for roughly 1,999,700 of those years. Only since the start of the Industrial Revolution has there been a big migration indoors. Today, the average urban worker in the United States only spends about five percent of their day in the open air. We are like caged animals.

Our bodies were not meant to be inside, seated in front of a screen all day. We didn't always work this way, of course. As hunter-gatherers and, later, as farmers, our ancestors relied on the outdoors. Nature wasn't just our playground; originally, it was where we worked. The advent of agricultural advances and the growth of cities enabled more labor to come together, which would supposedly improve efficiency.

In the early 1900s through the 1930s and '40s, spaces were highly regimented to maximize efficiency, with workers occupying rows upon rows of desks in a single large room where the managers sat at the perimeter to observe their employees. From the '40s to the late '70s, Franklin Lloyd Wright coined the open plan, which was considered a modern approach. By the '80s and '90s, we had moved onto the cubicle farm. The cubicles powered "action offices," a series of desks, workspaces, and other modular furniture designed to allow freedom of movement, and flexibility to work in a position suitable for the work being done (i.e., solo work on a computer). Many companies saw the modular dividers as a means to increase profitability. Offices full of cubicles became the norm.

## The Virtual Office

In the 1990s, one of the biggest developments was the increasing ease of internet access. The world wide web brought with it the development of an office phenomenon first seen at the turn of the twentieth century: widespread new technology—the internet, laptops, and mobile phones—could move offices, workers, and work away from the office and desk, and onto public transport, into homes and cafés.[1]

The recession of the early 1990s, combined with growing competition in increasingly globalized markets, put a squeeze on many businesses. Senior leaders could not ignore the cost savings of teleworking and outsourcing facilitated by advanced telecommunications. Growing land prices and ground rents in urban areas saw more and more multinational companies relocating out of city centers to industrial parks and underused land accessible only by small train stations and motorways.

## COVID-19: The Great Work from Home Experiment

In 2020, millions of organizations were forced to close their workplaces and switch to a full-time remote working model—many for more than a year. Despite initial fears about how organizations and workers would cope, the general consensus is that most adapted well initially.

As a collective, we began to ask what it meant to go to work. Geography no longer was the top priority. The virtual platform reigned. Many felt grateful that they were able to keep working, while also staying safe. The benefits included more time with family, less time commuting, and re-prioritizing what mattered.

---

[1] "The Evolution of Office Design," Morgan Lovell, accessed March 19, 2022, https://www.morganlovell.co.uk/the-evolution-of-office-design.

For some, especially busy entrepreneurs and business owners, this was the first time they had slowed down in *years*. They were taking calls on their patio. They actually had time for a lunch break.

Initially, workers freed from the supervision of their managers enjoyed the autonomy of home-working, but as the months went by they came to miss the social and collaborative opportunities the office environment offered. All that screen time left us feeling isolated. And because we are social beings, the prolonged physical separation brought anxiety, depression, and insomnia for many.

A survey of almost 200,000 people who worked from home showed that while their home environment enabled them to work productively, they missed social interaction and connection to their colleagues and the organization.[2] COVID-19 started to eat away at the very culture that organizations have spent years cultivating in their buildings, and which was always cited as a competitive differentiator.

Not only do endless online meetings and prolonged screen time *feel* worse, but the science now suggests that it tangibly *is* worse. One study released in May 2021 found that social isolation caused by lockdowns impairs cognitive function.[3] It makes people perform worse at basic problem-solving, learning new tasks, memory recall, time estimation, and more. So, where does that leave us?

---

[2] Ibid.

[3] Joanne Ingram, Christopher J. Hand, and Greg Maciejewski, "Social Isolation during COVID-19 Lockdown Impairs Cognitive Function," Wiley Online Library, March 17, 2021, https://onlinelibrary.wiley.com/doi/full/10.1002/acp.3821.

# LET'S MEET OUTSIDE

*"Nature holds the key to our aesthetic, intellectual, cognitive, and even spiritual satisfaction."*

—E.O. WILSON, AUTHOR OF BIOPHILIA

The solution—whether working from home or the office—is to conduct BusinessOutside. Post-pandemic, many remote workers happily chose to return to the office. It makes sense why they did. We have long known that the human mind relies on social connections to function properly. Face-to-face social contact maintains our mental and emotional health. During this time, many have also realized how important it is to get outside—to breathe the fresh air and move beyond four walls. Being out in nature can help us recharge so we don't feel depleted. Nature sparks authenticity, innovation, conversation, and connection. In my own life, countless ideas and meaningful relationships have been built from being on the trail. I have seen just how much meaning nature can add to our lives.

The BusinessOutside concept is about how to live and, yes, work in nature. But as we'll see, it's also about getting outside comfort zones, outside outdated corporate norms, and finding your true self. In short, it's a metaphor for doing things differently, and we'll return to this metaphor throughout the book.

\* \* \*

Meeting outside can feel like a foreign concept. I often get a lot of push-back when I tell people they don't need to be in a conference room to conduct business. There are picnic tables right outside. *What if it's too sunny?* All right. Let's pick the table up and move it under the tree. It sounds so simple and basic, but people have concerns that are easily solvable. *There are no wheels on the picnic table.* How many people does it take to pick it up? Three? Great. There are four of us. Let's just move the picnic table. *Are we allowed to move the picnic table?* Why wouldn't we be able to move the picnic table?

Most people just don't think like this; for years, they have been looking outside from their office window and pining. This speaks to a convention, a way in which something is usually done. They're all used to following the rules. They're used to working inside. They're programmed to think, "We can't have meetings outside!"

My question is: Why does it have to be that way?

If you get nothing else from this book, I want you to start to think of ways you can do things differently in your life. I'm not suggesting you completely turn your life upside down. (Unless your life needs a serious shake-up; then, by all means, go for it!) But you might be surprised to discover that by making a few minor adjustments in your daily routine, your sense of fulfillment increases significantly.

## Lead by Example

While it may feel implausible to suddenly change your routine, there are a number of ways you can apply the BusinessOutside concept.

Shortly after I moved to Boulder, I was asked to step in to lead a yoga, fitness, and wellness company. Naturally, the company offered yoga classes for employees throughout the day. I decided I would prioritize taking a yoga class at least three times a week for as long as I was there. Even though I was busy in my new role as president of the company, it was an intentional choice. I wanted to show the other employees that I could live the company's core values.

In my first class, I was so surprised to find only three other people. But over time, things began to change. The employees saw that the president was attending yoga classes, and that gave them the permission they needed to do the same. In the next class I attended, ten other employees showed up; the time after that, there were twenty people.

One day, when I was walking down the hall with my yoga mat, the CEO of the company made a comment as we passed. *"Oh, it must be nice."* I was startled by the comment. The subtext, of course, was that *it must be nice to have so much free time that you can take a yoga class during the day.* I was trying to lead by example, but instead the CEO made it seem that I must be shirking my responsibilities or not working as hard as she was. Even though the company *said* they had a culture of health, wellness, and balance, the reason there were no people in those early classes was because everyone knew that the actual corporate culture rewarded more hours behind the desk, and that employees should do yoga on their own time. Even though this culture was so strongly set, I kept doing yoga and even incorporated Walkie-Talkie meetings (more on those in a moment) with my colleagues and coworkers. Little by little, we began to change the corporate culture.

Like that CEO, many workers have the misconception that when they spend time outdoors, engage with movement at work, or do much of anything outside the norm, they aren't really working. In fact, according to a study conducted by outdoor retailer L.L. Bean, 92 percent of people only get outdoors for lunch or other breaks in the course of the workday.[4] Taking a break to decompress outside is certainly beneficial and can help rejuvenate your mind and emotional well-being, but actually working outside can do much more to increase productivity and creativity.

There are countless ways to do BusinessOutside. If you aren't sure where to start, use the following list as prompts:

1. **Book the outdoors.** Just like booking a room, make it possible to book the outdoor space—whether that's at the office or your remote workplace. Set up shop on your home patio, grab a picnic table, or bring a folding chair to a park.

2. **Walkie-Talkies.** These are one-on-one walking meetings outside. Ideally in-person. But if that's not possible, ditch the video call and tell your team to take their phones and start a walking meeting. Not only does it provide a built-in way to de-stress, but walking together creates a common bond, generates creativity and clarity, and is better for your physical and mental health than sitting behind your desk.

---

[4] "L.L. Bean: Be an Outsider at Work Handbook," https://www.llbean.com/shop/files/18 0619_HANDBOOK.pdf?nav=C12tX-517153, page 15.

3. **Weekly check-out.** Check-ins are typically a time for managers and employees to touch base and update one another. A check-out is an invitation to be outside at any time throughout the day. It can create an opportunity to be more open and talkative. I find that being outside is more efficient and creates richer conversations. Research shows us that 87 percent of people enjoy the outdoors and nearly 86 percent would like to spend more time outdoors during the workday.[5] So, schedule a check-out—either with teammates or by yourself.

4. **BusinessOutside brainstorm.** As mentioned, we often generate more and better ideas outside.[6] In a groundbreaking study, Stanford University researchers measured the effects of walking on problem solving and idea generation. Of all the variables tested, 81 percent of participants experienced enhanced creative thinking from walking outdoors.[7] Try taking the brainstorm outdoors and watch how many more ideas you can generate.

---

[5] Ibid.

[6] David Strayer, Ruth Ann Atchley, Paul Atchley, *Creativity in the Wild: Improving Creative Reasoning through Immersion in Natural Settings* (San Francisco: PLoS ONE, 2012). https://journals.plos.org/plosone/article/file?id=10.1371/journal.pone.0051474&type=printable

[7] Laura Brophy, "Incorporating Outdoor Space in the Work Environment: Designing for Long-term Impact," *WorkDesign Magazine*, accessed March 19, 2022, https://www.workdesign.com/2019/05/outdoor-workspace-designing-for-long-term-impact/.

5. **Fresh-Air Fridays.** Statistics show that 77 percent of people regularly eat lunch at their desk. L.L. Bean coined the term "Fresh-Air Fridays." Taking perks like catered lunches into the fresh air and having regularly scheduled picnics will break the routine and make lunch breaks even more healthy and fulfilling. Whether at the office or remote, take a Fresh-Air Friday. When I was at big companies like Kellogg's and Novartis, anytime there was a meeting with more than ten people, it was often scheduled over the lunch hour. If you're already doing that, why not take that meal into the fresh air?

6. **Power presentations.** Often, people sit inside a conference room when doing a dry run through slides and talking points. Did you know we remember more when we rehearse outside? Next time you find yourself preparing for an important presentation, rehearse it outside and make the most of the extra memory boost that nature offers.

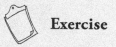 **Exercise**

In the next week, find one new way you can take Business Outside: conduct one of your meetings outside, book a weekly check-out, or a Fresh-Air Friday. Move the picnic table, get in the shade, have a meeting outside.

* * *

If more companies were made aware of the ways that working outside can bolster productivity and promote happiness, more workers would feel empowered to get outdoors. But the culture needs to change first, and that starts with the leaders. As a leader in your business, you have an opportunity to lead the way outside and establish a tighter team with more authentic connections and relationships as you do.

Two million years of evolution can't be wrong. Humans thrive outside.

CHAPTER TWO

# Challenging Conventional Wisdom

> *"Be willing to get fired for a good idea."*
>
> —SPIKE JONZE

THE AVERAGE EMPLOYEE SPENDS 90,000 HOURS—A THIRD OF THEIR life!—at work. If you have risen through the ranks at a large company, that number might be even higher. You're working ten to twelve hours a day, leaving little energy to do the things you value most with the people who matter most to you. You're not making time for yourself. Weekends speed by with family and friends. You are pulled in different directions and often feel so much pressure and many demands on your time.

You have achieved all the markers of what society deems successful, but you feel like life is happening to you instead of being designed by you. You feel caught in the rat race, chasing what you think is important. You may not even realize that you are going through the motions. You see people in other careers who have more personal freedom and you aspire to have that but don't know how to get out of your current daily grind.

You love your job, but something is missing. You might be feeling bored, stuck in the monotony of a mundane routine. This doesn't mean you're trapped; it means you're not leveraging the tools you need to shift into a more intentional life.

* * *

In the previous chapter, we looked at the importance of physically getting yourself and your team out in nature, and the benefits of doing that. Now it's time to explore ways to do business outside the corporate norms of conventional thinking. The truth is that you can actually be more nimble and agile when you move outside the box, but you have to be willing to take the first steps.

When I was working in the eye care division of Novartis, a global pharmaceutical company, I was responsible for selling contact lenses. I'll never forget being asked to breakfast by a senior VP of Marketing (let's call him Jeff). He had concerns about my working style and was upset that I was working on projects that involved his team without keeping him in the loop. I specifically remember him using the term "maverick" in a derogatory way. In the moment, I felt like I had done something wrong. Later, however, I couldn't help but smile, realizing that a maverick was exactly what I was: an unorthodox and independent-minded person—willing to challenge the status quo, without fear. Although he meant something much different when he used the word, I took it as a compliment. I was proud to be a maverick, and I knew my choices were actually benefiting the company, whether or not this executive could see that. Even in an environment like that, where I was expected to operate within the confines of the corporate structure, I experienced firsthand the positive results that come when you are willing to risk being innovative.

I heard a quote early in my career, and it has stayed with me. Steve Jobs famously said:

> I didn't see it then, but it turned out that getting fired from Apple was the best thing that could have happened to me. The heaviness of being successful was replaced by the lightness of being a beginner again, less sure about everything. It freed me to enter one of the most creative periods of my life.

What the quote meant to me was I had to take chances in order to make my mark. I have carried this concept with me to this day: be brave, challenge the status quo, and make bold moves...because that is where growth happens.

## MOVE FAST AND BREAK THINGS

Facebook founder, Mark Zuckerberg has a now-famous motto, "Move fast and break things." The idea is that if you aren't breaking things, you are delivering value too slowly.

In the summer of 2012, I was running SoloHealth, a company I had founded after leaving Novartis. The company was formed after a scribbled idea on a napkin would not leave me alone: *Create a tech company that empowers people to take charge of their health through interactive health kiosks.* Finally, I committed to the idea and took the first step by launching a vision-screening booth. Soon, we had full self-service kiosks up and running, which included screenings for blood pressure, weight and body mass index, and a health risk assessment, along with an interface that could locate nearby health care providers.

When Walmart called to say they were ready to scale, one of the contingencies of their agreement was that we had to obtain approval from the US Food and Drug Administration (FDA). This, they knew, would add the necessary safety, and credibility, to the offering. Concurrently, Dell had agreed to invest $25 million, but only if we had the Walmart agreement. It all hinged on this FDA approval.

The FDA required that we test one hundred consumers to obtain approval. Somewhere along the way, we miscalculated, and realized after the fact that we had only tested fifty. It had been a long and involved process just to get these fifty people, and we had already spent thousands of dollars and months of time in recruitment and testing.

We were running out of cash, and we had to move quickly. To come up with a solution, we brainstormed different ways to have an additional fifty people go through our blood pressure kiosk and then be tested in a hospital environment. We needed to prove that our blood pressure cuff was consistently as accurate as a medical-grade cuff operated by a trained medical professional.

And then the idea came to me. What if we could intercept consumers in a location where there is a lot of foot traffic, like in a mall, and have their blood pressure taken on the spot? One of our regular lunch spots was a place called Jack's Deli, which happened to be next door to an empty retail space. A "Space for Lease" sign hung on the door, which included a phone number. It struck me that this was exactly what we were looking for: lots of open space in a high-traffic area. We moved three kiosks into that retail space for the afternoon.

Next, I went to the fire station and asked if I could buy lunch for a couple of their certified EMTs to act as our trained medical professionals. They gladly agreed.

At Jack's Deli, we bought fifty $10 gift cards. I had two people on my team intercept diners as they were entering the deli. We let them know we were doing some testing and asked if they would mind getting their blood pressure taken. We told them it would only take ten minutes and they would get a free lunch as compensation. They looked at us like it was too good to be true, and sure enough we quickly reached our fifty. They used the gift card to buy their lunch and then came next door to see us.

We had each person sit down in one of the kiosks to have their blood pressure tested while the EMT from the fire station sat in the corner. In three hours, we ran fifty people through the kiosks and had the test results signed off by a qualified EMT. Our technical team reviewed the data to make sure our results were as good as the results from the EMT measurements. We FedEx'ed the results to the FDA, and within three weeks had the approval we needed.

If we had acted like many companies, we would have needed three weeks simply to coordinate a meeting to talk about how to solve the problem. Had we followed conventional wisdom, we would have needed to involve the regulatory division, corporate compliance, and the communications team. Once we finally got to the meeting, we would need to hire a recruiting firm. We would have had to develop a new set of protocols, which would have easily taken another month or two. Another few weeks would be spent recruiting patients. Each patient would be given fifty to a hundred dollars for their participation, while the recruiting firm would be paid double that or more.

In total, it would have taken a minimum of six months to follow conventional protocols. We would have risked losing both deals with Dell and Walmart in the process. Instead, we were able to bypass that bureaucracy and accomplish our goal in one afternoon, *simply by challenging conventional wisdom*.

Challenging conventional wisdom starts with reassessing and asking two key questions:

## 1. What Problem Are You Trying to Solve?

In our case, the answer was to check the box to satisfy the FDA's requirement. We needed to test the blood pressure of fifty more people so that we could prove our blood pressure cuff was as accurate as an EMT using a conventional blood pressure machine. I could never have bypassed protocol like this inside most big companies. What I hope you get from this story is that you can get results faster;

you just have to think differently. Move fast, fix things, and be willing to break the rules.

## 2. Are You Willing to be Accountable for Your Actions?

You have to be willing to fall on your sword. I was always ready and willing to explain what we were doing and why, if or when a boss questioned my motives or actions. In this scenario, I would have easily been able to make a case about why we needed to move fast. Bottom line, results always trump a little transgression. Fifty people got a free lunch, we stayed on budget, we solved the problem, and we got the task done.

Too often, we don't take risks because we are afraid of being reprimanded or getting in trouble. Nine times out of ten, no one cares as long as you get the job done. You, too, can be more nimble and agile to move both yourself and your organization forward. You don't have to quit your job or blow up your entire career. All I'm suggesting here is that you identify opportunities where you can get clear on your desired outcomes and key objectives, and find a way to achieve them in an inventive way. This alone can lead you to a more intentional work life.

## THE FIVE WHYS

When I was managing a team, I found a great way to motivate them to move fast and be more innovative was through a technique called the Five Whys, which taps into the cause-and-effect relationships underlying a particular problem.

I first learned about the Five Whys technique while doing a brainstorming "blitz" with SolveNext, a San Francisco-based firm focused on facilitation and corporate innovation. The technique was developed by Taiichi Ohno, pioneer of the Toyota Production System in the 1950s. He instructed the team to "ask 'why' five times about every matter."[8]

To use this strategy, start with your problem and ask the question "why" approximately five times to drill into each answer and ultimately identify the root cause of the original problem.[9]

**An example of a problem is:** The vehicle will not start.

1. *Why?*—The battery is dead. (First why)

2. *Why?*—The alternator is not functioning. (Second why)

3. *Why?*—The alternator belt has broken. (Third why)

4. *Why?*—The alternator belt was well beyond its useful service life and not replaced. (Fourth why)

5. *Why?*—The vehicle was not maintained according to the recommended service schedule. (Fifth why, a root cause.)

---

[8] Taiichi Ohno, "Ask 'Why' Five Times about Every Matter," Toyota, March 2006, https://www.toyota-myanmar.com/about-toyota/toyota-traditions/quality/ask-why-five-times-about-every-matter.

[9] Olivier Serrat, "The Five Whys Technique," Knowledge Solutions, February 2009, https://www.adb.org/publications/five-whys-technique.

As I managed the team, I began to get to the root of what caused a block in the process. We could then use this understanding to move forward in a better way. For example, I was frequently given protracted timelines to complete simple tasks, and I wasn't sure why. So, the next time I was told a task was going to take two weeks, I started asking why. Only by understanding the root of the issue could I then provide a solution to help prioritize the task.

1. *Why is the deadline so far in the future?* **Answer:** "I am spending 30 percent of my day on tasks that pull focus, such as commuting and meetings."

2. *Why can't this task be completed by the end of the week?* **Answer:** "I can't do this with all the distractions here."

3. *Why do you have to be here? What if you could work from home and save commuting time?* **Answer:** "That would help, but I need to be in the office because I have three meetings scheduled this week, and they are affecting my ability to meet my deliverables."

4. **Why** do you need to attend those meetings this week? Can they be canceled or rescheduled? What if you could skip those three meetings? **Answer:** "Yes, that would help, but I have other tasks to complete in addition to this task."

5. **Why** haven't you asked for help with these tasks? What if you did not have these other tasks on your plate? What if I asked a team member to take one of these tasks off

your plate? **Answer:** "Oh, I could get it done in two days." Great. So how about we give you five days?

*To use this strategy, you may not always need to ask why five times.* What is important is to get down to the root of our actions. In the corporate environment, people are used to the motions—doing things the way that they have always been done, without thinking about *why they're doing them that way.* If you keep asking why, you can finally understand the real issue, which allows you to then come up with a simple solution quickly.

## UNLEASH THE POWER OF UNCONVENTIONAL THINKING

I met Carla soon after she had taken over as global head of professional affairs for a Fortune 500 company. The company had 110 associates worldwide, and she was in charge of bringing together two groups that had been siloed but were now sharing resources.

Carla was new to the role, replacing someone with a poor reputation for building trust. There were communication barriers and multiple other challenges in her department, so she asked me to facilitate a three-day summit at the company headquarters in Dallas.

Carla really didn't know where to begin, so I had her start by outlining her key objectives and her desired outcome. I asked: *What do you want people to think, feel, and do at the end of the summit?* One of her key objectives was to build trust among the team and align key priorities in order to create a clear understanding of their roles, responsibilities, and measurable goals.

When you don't know where to begin, start by outlining:

1. Key objectives
2. Desired outcome

In other words, what do you want people to think, feel, and do?

I challenged Carla to think three steps ahead, knowing what a big opportunity this was for her and the company. This kind of undertaking had never been done before in the professional affairs group. I knew we had to capture this unprecedented occasion: 110 associates from all over the globe together for the first time. Between sessions, I coached Carla behind the scenes, and she found several ways to maximize her impact along the way. The summit exceeded our expectations.

On the last day, we gathered everyone to take a picture, and an idea popped into my head. That night I said, "You know, tomorrow is the last day. Make an announcement that you are going to post this on LinkedIn and that you would like everyone else to tag themselves and share the photo."

Carla replied, "Oh, no, we can't do that." She had been trained on corporate compliance and knew what the company allowed in terms of public communication. Social media sharing wasn't allowed.

"Excuse me?" I said. "That can't be the case." But Carla was adamant there was no way. I didn't want to give up so easily, so I asked to talk to someone in corporate communications. Carla agreed to invite the right person to the meeting the following day.

The next day, I pulled the corporate communications person aside before the meeting and told him what we were planning to do. He was somewhat open to it but still wanted to go through several layers of approvals first. He wanted to email one person and copy two others. Then he would have to go through a committee before getting approval.

"We don't have time for that," I said. "It's going to go out today." Carla and her colleague both looked at me like I was from Mars. "Guys," I continued, "the world is changing. It's happening fast. And we can't keep doing the things that we've done. We've got to think differently. We've got to move faster. The fact is there was a meeting that was held today with 110 professionals from all over the world. We are proud and excited about the future and what we are building together. We are aligned, and we're focused. Those are facts. That's happening. And not being able to share that is doing a disservice to your department and to the company."

After some convincing, they finally warmed up to the idea. I offered to draft the LinkedIn post for Carla and wrote out something simple like: *I'm proud and excited to lead the first ever global Professional Affairs Summit.* Carla posted it on her account and tagged all the executive leaders who were in that meeting, adding a couple of hashtags. Finally, she tagged the company.

At this point, Carla was definitely doing business outside her comfort zone. She called me and said, "Okay, I'm getting ready to hit send. I'm really nervous." She explained that she was especially worried that somebody in corporate compliance was going to slap her wrist and tell her she couldn't do that, and make her take the post down.

"That's the worst that could happen?" I asked. "Isn't it worth trying?" After a few long minutes, Carla hit send, and sure enough the opposite of her fears took place.

People loved the post. In fact, it went viral. Not only did it elevate the company, but it also elevated her department. One of the themes and taglines that was created as a result of the summit was, "Unleash the power of professional affairs." Part of unleashing that power was telling people who the professional affairs department was and what they did. The team had done some amazing things, but no one knew about them. A simple LinkedIn post helped change that.

From that point forward, everything shifted for Carla and her role within the organization. Her boss had an acknowledgment system called "Weekly Kapow moments" and she won the Kapow award for getting herself out there and promoting the organization. Carla took the small risk of reprimand and it paid off.

Unconventional thinking often works this way. At first, it feels scary. After all, you're going outside the standards you've known. But once you take that step, more times than not, you reap rewards you could have never imagined. I've seen this happen time and time again.

## Think Outside the Cereal Box

I saw the power of unconventional thinking play out in a completely different way when I worked at Kellogg's in the late '90s. At the time, Kellogg's had won Marriott's business to supply cereal for all of their hotels worldwide. Everyone in the company was talking about the deal because General Mills, a large competitor, had retained Marriott's business for ten years up to that point. We could only imagine how much of our cereal would now be sold in hotels across the world.

As the story goes, General Mills was so angry about losing the hotel chain's business that the CEO sent a group voicemail to all of their salespeople worldwide. The voicemail said something to the effect of, "As you may be aware, Kellogg's was awarded the Marriott business. We are a large client of Marriott's. We all stay in Marriott properties worldwide...thousands of us every night." Then he said, "The next time you check out of your Marriott hotel, when they ask you how your stay went, say, 'Great, but you didn't have Cheerios.' Don't tell them who you are. Don't tell them you're with General Mills. Just say, 'I missed having my Cheerios.'"

Within two days, more than one hundred complaints were filed about the lack of Cheerios at breakfast through Marriott international. Within three weeks, Marriott had to call Kellogg's and get a *carve-out* not only for Cheerios, but for three other products as well, because they perceived that there was a frenzied outcry by Marriott customers for General Mills' products. Of course, Marriott had no idea these complaints were all filed by General Mills' employees. What was especially genius about the strategy was that the employees weren't lying; everything they were saying was true. They *did* want Marriott to carry Cheerios.

Sure enough, the unconventional plan worked. Within weeks, Cheerios were back.

## Meeting within a Meeting

Another way to use unconventional thinking and move outside the norm is to run "meetings within meetings." It's a simple strategy: to leverage an existing gathering to meet with like-minded people about a topic that is important to them. But the benefits are exponential.

I learned just how creative you can be with meetings within meetings when I attended The Vision Council's annual Executive Summit, an event open to all executives in the eye care industry. By that point, I had been in the eye care industry for twenty years and was a well-connected and experienced leader, so I thought the organizers would share my vision: to host forum groups that facilitated meaningful, rich, authentic discussions. Unfortunately, they declined my offer. But I didn't take their no as a final no.

When I arrived in Florida for the summit, I noticed that a buffet breakfast was planned at eight o'clock the next morning. I texted twelve of the top executives already attending the summit—CEOs whom I knew were willing to go beyond surface-level conversations —and wrote, *You belong to a unique group of CEOs at the Summit who have a growth mindset and are willing to share. I'm hosting breakfast tomorrow where we will share thoughts, ideas, and best practices. I'd love you to come. Please make sure to arrive by 7:45.*

Sure, this was the same breakfast event everyone else was attending; I was simply inviting this group to sit at my table and participate in a facilitated discussion. I arrived at 7:30 while the buffet was still being set up. I took a moment to thank the venue manager for setting everything up, and she assumed I was an event organizer. I chose the middle table at the very front of the room. My group, the who's who of the summit, were all there with me, front and center. I smiled as everyone at the conference looked on, wondering what was going on at our table.

We shared "needs and leads," and each member had an opportunity to ask peers for help: something they were stuck on, a problem keeping them up at night, or a connection they were looking to make. The rest of the group shared their firsthand experiences and offered a solution or resources. It was one of the most rewarding experiences of the entire summit.

Throughout these stories, you've probably noticed a pattern. Being unwilling to take no as an answer allows you to cut through conventional thinking and find a new way forward. But that's not the only way to take the unconventional route in business. Sometimes, frontline innovation is the best way to challenge the status quo.

## FRONTLINE INNOVATION

To move like an innovator, you have to find creative ways to tap into resources you don't yet have. This is exactly what Dennis Steadman did in 2011.

You might be familiar with Frontline, a popular flea and tick protection product for dogs. The patent for Frontline is owned by a company called Merial. In year fifteen of the seventeen-year-long patent, Steadman approached Walmart and let them know he was going to create a competing product, a private label called PetArmor.

His company, Valcera, offered to give Walmart a 10 percent share equity in their company. They did not need any cash; PetArmor offered Walmart exclusivity for two years in exchange for guaranteed orders, marketing support, and access to Walmart's vast team of in-house lawyers, so that they would be at the ready if and when they were sued. A suit certainly wasn't out of the question; Merial was a huge company, and PetArmor was tiny.

There were a number of contingencies, but Valcera ended up getting Walmart to commit. They took that agreement to a venture capital firm in New York and raised $49 million to build the company. In two years, Merial went from a 70 percent market share down to 60, and then down to 50. On the other hand, PetArmor, built on the back of Walmart, skyrocketed. The company sold three years later for $160 million.[10]

The innovators of PetArmor not only took an unconventional approach, but they also overtook the conventional competitor in the market. They circumvented all of the traditional red tape by

---

[10] "Perrigo Acquisition of Velcera, Inc—Known for its PetArmor® Franchise of Flea and Tick Treatments—Closes Today," Cision, April 1, 2013, https://www.prnewswire.com/news-releases/perrigo-acquisition-of-velcera-inc----known-for-its-petarmor-franchise-of-flea-and-tick-treatments----closes-today-200877311.html

going right to the top. Could you do the same in your business or with your new idea?

## Thousands of Rakes

While the story of PetArmor is insightful and inspiring, the truth is that frontline innovation doesn't usually require so much risk. It simply requires you to carry a simple idea forward.

In 2010, an entrepreneur named Rich Grange was watching news coverage of the British Petroleum (BP) oil spill in the Gulf of Mexico. On a Friday afternoon, the CEO of BP held a press conference, during which he promised to reimburse the city of New Orleans to clean up the beaches, and to "spare no expense" in doing so. Grange saw an opportunity here. He realized, "Well, if BP is going to spare no expense, perhaps I can capitalize on this."

Grange wasn't in the "beach cleanup" business, not by a long shot, but that didn't stop him; he'd find a way to access the resources he needed. First, he decided to buy thousands of rakes. Next, he approached his business partner with the idea. His partner had a staffing company, and the company could contract thousands of workers at a time to do jobs like Mardi Gras cleanup. On Monday morning, Grange approached BP and said, "I've got the crew and the rakes and everything we need. We can start tomorrow."

The city had been planning on sending out a Request for Proposal, but they ended up awarding the project to Grange because he had all the resources in place to make it easy for them to say yes. This quick thinking and fast action meant he ended up clearing a couple million dollars because BP had an immediate need to get it off their plate, and he was able to marshal these resources in an effective way.

If you take nothing else from this chapter, my hope is that you see that it can cost nothing to be innovative, and it doesn't have to take a lot of time, either. Yes, you *can* move fast and break things at the same time.

\* \* \*

All of these stories illustrate the myriad of ways you can set yourself apart from the crowd to achieve results. Because Carla was willing to take a risk, she was recognized and promoted in her role. People in the company started seeing her as a leader, and she ultimately became a worldwide corporate spokesperson.

Because of our innovative approach to offer $10 gift cards in exchange for a blood pressure test, we were able to get FDA approval within two weeks, which secured our deals with both Walmart and Dell. That one move completely transformed our business.

I started BusinessOutside because I was willing to challenge the status quo and think outside the box.

What about you? How will you challenge the status quo and think outside the box? How might moving beyond conventional wisdom change your business and your life?

# CHAPTER THREE

# Establishing Deeper Level Connections

> *"You will find as you look back upon your life that the moments that stand out, the moments when you have really lived, are the moments when you have done things in a spirit of love."*
>
> —HENRY DRUMMOND

GROWING UP, I GOT TO SEE HOW HARD MY DAD WORKED TO RUN his own business, Foster Financial Services, where he sold insurance for one of the large insurance brokers. I witnessed firsthand his dedication to community, making connections, bringing people together, and having genuine empathy for others. Even in a room of one hundred people, he always made you feel like you were the only one in the room.

My admiration for my dad propelled me to reluctantly agree when he suggested I have lunch with one of his good friends, George, on an upcoming trip to Chicago. It was the summer after I graduated college, and this successful businessman was a fraternity brother my dad had known for thirty years.

I remember rolling my eyes and asking why I would want to have lunch with this crusty old guy.

"It's really important to me," my dad said. "I think it will be a good connection for you."

I felt awkward because I didn't know what we'd talk about. "Just ask him for advice," my dad said.

"Advice about what?"

He looked at me and said, "Son, it doesn't matter. Ask him for advice about anything. Perhaps say, 'Looking back to when you were twenty years old, knowing what you know now, what would you do differently?'"

So that's exactly what I did.

At lunch, I explained the business path I was on, and George told me to try to work overseas if I ever had the opportunity. He told me to lay my foundation by exposing myself to as many different people and departments as I could early in my career. To learn sales and marketing. To understand how the product team runs.

"It's like building scaffolding," he said. "It doesn't matter as much what the job is, as long as you're learning." He highlighted that taking these actions would help me stand out as a potential hire.

His suggestions turned out to be good advice.

When I got back home, I told my dad all about our conversation.

"Great!" he replied. "Now I'd like you to write George a thank you note and share with him some of the ideas he gave you." I probably rolled my eyes again. But I said I would, and I did.

Six months later, when I came home for Thanksgiving, Dad referenced that lunch again. "I'd like you to write to George one more time," he said. "I think it's really important that he understands where you are in your career." By that time, I had taken a job at Kellogg's that I was excited about, and Dad recommended I share the news with his friend.

At first, I was reluctant. *Write yet another letter?* I thought. Then my dad gave me the book, *Dig Your Well Before You're Thirsty* by Harvey Mackay. The premise of that book is that it's important to build relationships long before you need them. The biggest thing that resonated with me in the book was the concept that *a network never sleeps.* To this day, that is still a guiding concept in my life.

In the book, Mackay tells a story about one of his friends who had gotten a call at two in the morning from someone he hadn't talked to in more than ten years. The caller was semi-hysterical because his accountant had called him that afternoon and told him he was broke; his company couldn't make payroll, and if he didn't retrieve the checks he'd written, there was a good chance he would go to jail. He needed $20,000. Well, Mackay's friend offered to lend him a few thousand dollars, but he didn't give him all he needed *even though he could have.* Why? Because the connection just wasn't there anymore. Not only did this 2:00 a.m. caller not dig his well before he was thirsty, he waited until he was dying of thirst before he even broke ground.

I got the point. I wouldn't be able to call someone I hadn't talked to in ten years out of the blue and say, "Hey, you know, I have a family emergency, something really bad happened. Can you wire me twenty grand?" The person on the other end of the line wouldn't feel any sense of connection to the need. And they'd likely be living a completely different life than they were before.

Mackay goes on to ask how many people you could call and ask for $20,000 at 2:00 a.m. For most people, it's two, maybe three. Mackay shares that he has at least fifty people he could call because he invested so much into his relationships and provided so much value for the people in his life, long before he needed anything from them. Now, they would do anything for him.

With Mackay's words in the back of my head, I decided to take my dad's advice and continue building my network of connections one step at a time. I wrote George that letter, and that simple action started me on a path toward building deeper, more meaningful connections. I decided I wanted fifty people I could call on, too, and now I have more than that. It's no surprise that the majority of the opportunities that have come my way are because of relationships I have cultivated over the years with people all over the world.

Through that process—meeting my dad's friend and reading the Harvey Mackay book—I realized two things: one, people love to give advice; and, two, allowing others to contribute to my journey builds a deeper connection because they now have a vested interest in my success. I started asking more people for advice and following up with them over and over again in my own life. As I built those relationships, I had more and more people cheering me on from the sidelines. My successes contributed to *their* sense of fulfillment and satisfaction. They were vested in my life because they had given me a small piece of themselves. If they had contributed—even only a little—it was a win-win. And I went about creating as many win-wins as I could.

## FOCUS ON BUILDING RELATIONSHIPS

In those early days, I remember thinking that I wanted to develop what Harvey Mackay called a "deep network." My thinking has evolved since then, and today networking is almost a dirty word. I myself have a visceral reaction to it because so many people do it wrong. Networking has become very superficial. Those base conversations about what you do, how your job is going, and the weather are mind-numbing and boring. No one wants to get caught in a sea of mindless chit-chat. And when they do, you can see their eyes darting around the cocktail reception, looking for a way to break free and find the next person to talk to.

I like to reframe networking and focus instead on actually building authentic relationships. When I go into a cocktail reception, I know well in advance what my goal is: usually, there are two or three people with whom I want to have a meaningful conversation. I want to develop a deep connection that goes beyond the superficial stuff.

People at networking events are often there for their own purposes; they want your business, they want referrals, they want *something*, and the communication often reflects that. It's not about getting to know you or establishing that deeper connection. I've learned that approaching these events the opposite way is actually a lot more beneficial in the long run. I go into each conversation wondering how I can help the other person. Turns out, Harvey Mackay and my dad were right; help others before they ever ask for something, and you'll build meaningful relationships that make your business and life that much richer.

I try to end almost every conversation by asking, "How can I help?" Most people are pleasantly surprised by the question. Most will reciprocate and often figure out a way that *they* can help me, even though that is not the purpose of my question. This is the law of reciprocity at work, a concept popularized by Robert Cialdini in his book *Influence: The Psychology of Persuasion*. People, by nature, treat others as they have been treated. Psychology explains this by stressing that humans simply hate to feel indebted to others.[11]

Every once in a while, someone will ask for something—perhaps an introduction, a connection, a speaking opportunity, a good book to read—and every time I do whatever I can to fulfill that request, because I know that I'm digging my well before I'm thirsty, and it feels good to help. I never know when that will come back—if ever —but I have countless examples of times a true connection with someone helped open up a job opportunity, or tickets to the Super Bowl, or new business ideas. All because I cultivated those relationships years in advance.

---

[11] Robert B. Cialdini, *Influence: The Psychology of Persuasion* (New York City: Harper Business, 2006).

The art of building relationships before you need them is only step one; it's the most superficial aspect of relationship building. After this step, you must continue investing in each relationship to deepen connection and build trust.

There are some simple strategies you can implement to go the extra mile and show people you are interested in getting to know them. Taking the time at the very beginning of a relationship will make the difference. These simple steps apply to building relationships in business and the rest of life as well.

## Learn Names

> *"It's not that you forgot. You just didn't take the time to remember."*
>
> —HARRY LORAYNE, MEMORY-TRAINING MASTER

The first step in establishing deeper level connections is to learn and remember people's names. Make an effort to learn a name the very first time you meet them.

I'm sure you've been in social situations where you have a neighbor that moves in. You might ask their name the first two or three times, but once they have lived there any longer than that—five or six months—and you still don't know, it becomes awkward. It comes across as insensitive not to have taken the time to learn it.

The same goes with teams and coworkers. When somebody first joins your team, you have the unique opportunity to get as much information from them as you can. Open up and be vulnerable, share, be empathetic, understand where they're coming from, and try to learn all about them. Take notes and establish that deep connection early. If you wait too long to take this step, it becomes more difficult.

## 4, 3, 2, 1

If you have ever found yourself at a networking event struggling to connect with the person you're speaking with, or find it challenging to get beyond small talk, a technique I have used very effectively is called 4, 3, 2, 1. In short, you want to have 4 stories, 3 facts, 2 quotes, and 1 question ready at all times. You may not actually share all of these in every conversation, but having them ready to share eliminates the awkward silence in conversation and invites the other person to share more about themselves as well.

**4 Stories:** Humans are hardwired to remember stories. Not only does telling a story let the other person get to know you, but when told well, it makes you memorable. Of the four stories you have ready to tell, one should be personal, one business, one should demonstrate a challenge, and the other should demonstrate a time you were successful.

**3 Facts:** Think about three facts you are passionate about, that are not widely known, and that you think are pertinent and relevant to the kinds of people you speak with on a regular basis.

**2 Quotes:** Memorize two quotes that inspire you and know who said them. Sharing these can be inspiring and even prompt further conversation.

**1 Question:** The question should be one you can ask to anyone in the world. This could be a billionaire, or it could be a homeless person on the street. The question I like to ask is, "Knowing what you know now, if you had to do it over, what would you tell yourself twenty years ago?"

Having 4 stories, 3 facts, 2 quotes, and 1 question as talking points allow you to be prepared for any cocktail reception conference, trade show, or event where you will be meeting new people. By genuinely sharing the emotion behind each of these, and why they matter to you will go a long way in helping you develop better relationships and more quickly build rapport with people.

## Ask the Right Questions

Each person is unique. This is a simple statement, but the more you show genuine interest in your coworkers, your neighbors, your friends, and even your family members, the more likely they are to open up and trust you. Start with questions. What are their personal values? What are their strengths and abilities? Understanding another person's true motivations can lead to a deeper level of trust. Knowing where others are coming from, and what makes them tick, allows you to better react and respond to their needs.

One of the questions I love to ask when I am in a conversation is, *What is giving you energy right now?* It's very open-ended, but when I can understand what matters to people personally, professionally, and in their family life, I know how I might be able to help that person in specific ways.

On the business front, the more I can help a person achieve their goals, the more buy-in I will get as their leader. This is a give-first mentality. Helping someone will make them want to reciprocate. Other go-to questions include:

- What brings you joy?
- What is keeping you up at night?
- Who is a person who made a big impact on your life?

## Handwritten Notes

When I first started at Novartis, I spent a few weeks rotating through various departments to learn more about the company. As a global pharmaceutical company, there was a lot to learn. During training, a customer service specialist spent three hours showing me how Novartis' customer service operates. Afterwards I wrote a short note to say thank you, expressing how much I appreciated her taking the time to help me get up to speed. A year later, I passed by the woman's desk who had provided the training, and she had the card I wrote pinned up on her bulletin board. It touched me so much, because it had taken such a small amount of my time—no more than twenty seconds to write—but was so special that she still had it pinned up a year later.

I realized then how much it matters to people when I take the time to show support and genuine gratitude. When I used to attend a lot of conferences, I would try to tap into the power of handwritten notes whenever possible. When I knew some prospects and clients were staying in the same hotel, I'd send them handwritten letters. Of course, the gesture stood out. After all, how often does somebody at the hotel bring an envelope or a small package to your room or call and say there is an envelope waiting for you downstairs? Each time someone received a letter from me at a hotel, they'd be surprised and delighted. I knew they'd remember that letter for a long time.

Later, when I started running my own company, I continued the tradition of letter writing. I would conduct the typical exit interview when an employee left the company, but I would also write them a handwritten note, even if they didn't report to me. I wished them well and always took the opportunity to ask if there was anything I could do to help. I would maintain those connections in the years to come, knowing it's a small world. So many of those people would show up as executives in different jobs, companies, and industries down the road, and we'd end up doing business again. That early effort to build a connection went a long way.

## The Personal Touch

Other ways to show up for people vary based on who the person is and who they are in your life, but it's often easy to create that special touch. I remember speaking with a colleague once who happened to mention that it was his twentieth wedding anniversary. Toward the end of the conversation, I circled back around and asked where they were going to dinner. Later, I called the maître d' and ordered a bottle of wine and sent my congratulations. He had forgotten that he had even told me the name of the restaurant. I took the opportunity that presented itself, and it went a long way in building a deeper connection with my colleague.

With the advent of technology, people don't give out business cards as much, so it's hard to reach them except by phone or email. Still, you can find ways to creatively connect. For example, I like sending a meaningful video text instead of email just to have that personal touch.

### Short Video Messages

One way I like to stay in contact with my community is via short video messages through text, or video messaging apps like WhatsApp, Voxer, or Marco Polo. I leave a personalized video telling them why I am thinking of them at that moment.

This is an effective way to connect with the people in your life and let them know you're thinking about them. There's something about hearing the sound of someone's voice, the emotion and inflection, that doesn't come across in a text message or an email. For me, there is an added benefit of creating a gratitude loop. More often than not, my message prompts further conversation ("I haven't heard from you in ages!").

## HOW TO CLEAR ISSUES

Establishing deeper level connections requires maintenance and upkeep. Much like caring for a home or for your car, you want to take care of issues as they arise, not letting things fester. By taking care of small issues, you keep them from becoming big ones.

The "clearing model" is a way to protect your relationships by providing a framework to have open and honest conversations and to restore balance. Authentic, clear communication is the secret.

In his book, *The Four Agreements*, Don Miguel Ruiz talks about the unnecessary drama and "emotional poison" we create for ourselves, our relationships, and our businesses when we don't have honest, clear communication. He writes, "We take things personally, we misunderstand, then we make assumptions, and we end up creating a whole big drama and suffering for nothing. We make all sorts of assumptions because we don't have the courage to ask questions." This happens all the time in business, and it's preventable. Practices like the clearing model alleviate drama.

Even when you've developed a good connection with someone, issues will still arise at some point. While it can be uncomfortable to confront issues and differences, doing so will strengthen your relationships over the long term.

In 2021, I was leading an in-person workshop and establishing the ground rules with the seven people attending, who comprised the company's executive leadership team. As we discussed what we wanted to accomplish in the following two days, the general consensus was that our goal was to have open and honest conversations and for each person to ask for what they wanted. Upon hearing this, one of the participants, Steve, jumped in and began addressing his coworker, Claire.

Steve said, "Claire, I cannot wait one more second. I've got to share with you that it is so annoying when you come to our weekly virtual management meeting while you're on your treadmill desk, bouncing up and down." Everyone laughed, except for Steve.

It was an awkward moment, but I used it as an opportunity to teach the clearing model to the group. It's a model that I use for myself and with clients to approach situations in which a connection is in jeopardy. It can be used in business and the workplace, for personal situations, family matters, and really in any environment or scenario in which miscommunication or a misunderstanding occurs.

Before beginning this process, make sure that the discussion happens at an appropriate time, that there won't be any distractions, and the individual has the time to speak. In this case, we were working on determining overall goals for the retreat, but Steve saw it as an opportunity to address a longstanding issue that had been bothering him. So, I went with it and began guiding the group through the exercise.

The following is an outline of the exercise you can use at any time to clear an issue.

Before you begin, it is important to *affirm* that your relationship with the other person is important. Next, *confirm* that there is an issue to clear, and make sure that now is a good time to have the conversation. If one person would rather talk about the issue later, it's important to respect that request and find a better time.

When both people are ready, the first step is to state the facts.

**Step 1: State the facts.** What are the facts of the situation that cannot be refuted?

This is meant to clarify things, so there is no misunderstanding about the issue being cleared. In this case, the facts were that: *Every week the group had a Zoom meeting, during which Claire was on a treadmill exercising.*

**Step 2: Identify the story you are telling yourself.** What is the story you have in your head (which may or may not be true) about the situation or dynamic at hand?

We often make assumptions that may or may not be true. It's important that the other person understands the perception we have in our head or the judgment we were making about the facts.

*Steve was telling himself that Claire thought she was so above everyone else that she could exercise whenever she wanted, and that neither he nor this meeting were important to her.*

**Step 3: Share how you feel.** What are the emotions or feelings tied to this situation?

You want the other person to understand how it makes you feel because they probably don't know.

*Steve needed to explain that he felt annoyed, distracted, and disrespected.*

**Step 4: Know your role.** What did you do (or not do) that contributed to this situation or dynamic?

It's important to take accountability for what you are responsible for in this issue.

*Claire had been doing this for a year. Steve knew he probably should have brought it up a long time ago but felt silly addressing it. He let it fester.*

**Step 5: Say what you want.** Determine what you want from the other person involved and state it clearly.

Communicating your needs will help you come to a resolution.

*It took us a few rounds back and forth before Steve finally admitted that he wanted Claire to stop exercising on the treadmill during the weekly call.*

When using the clearing model, it's important that the other person can mirror back what they heard. You want the person sharing the issue to know they have been heard, and give them an opportunity to share more if appropriate and necessary.

At this point in the process, Claire repeated back to Steve what she had heard.

She said, "If I heard you correctly, the facts are, we have a weekly management call and I am always on my treadmill desk during the Zoom call. The story you are telling yourself is that this meeting is not important to me and it makes you feel disrespected and annoyed. You believe your role is that you could have brought this issue up months ago, and what you want is for me to stop using my treadmill during the call. Is that right? Is there anything else?"

Steve acknowledged this was everything and that he had been heard. At this point, Claire was able to respond.

"I'm so glad you brought this up to me because I had no idea that it was so annoying. I was trying to multitask, and I thought I was being effective. I have two small kids and sometimes it's difficult for me to fit in my exercise outside of work. That said, if you're annoyed, maybe other people are, too. So, I'm going to commit to not using my treadmill desk during weekly meetings."

Steve confirmed that Claire had heard what he was saying, and that he had heard her in turn. Both Steve and Claire agreed that they were clear.

If either party is still not clear, the process is repeated. The matter isn't "cleared" until it is resolved. It is important that both sides are clear before completing the exercise; if one is but one isn't, the situation will continue unresolved.

Sometimes the process takes a few rounds. In some cases, you might hear the other person but simply not agree to what they want. It's one thing to voice an aggravation; it's another to figure out how to move forward together. This will vary from person to person and situation to situation. The clearing model is a starting point to understanding each other's point of view. Often, what needs to be cleared seems minor but affects people on a personal level. Exercising on a treadmill doesn't seem like a big deal, and it didn't actually impact Claire's work performance. The problem was that it caused annoyance and was distracting. So, when the issue was left unaddressed, it had the opportunity to breed resentment. And a team can only be so effective when members are annoyed by each other.

Once you know the clearing model, you don't have to go through all of the steps methodically. Instead, you can simply have an open conversation and really hear each other out, now that you know the required elements. I had this kind of conversation a couple of years ago, with a really good friend of mine, Brent, after failing to address a misunderstanding for more than a decade. Resentment had built up over time, and our relationship was strained, but neither of us brought up the issue.

One day, Brent finally opened up and told me, "I really value our relationship, and I never want anything to come between us. That said, there's something that has been eating at me for years. And I want to clear some things."

"Great. I'd love to work through it," I replied. I knew Brent was familiar with the clearing model, so I asked if he'd be up for sharing through that lens, and he agreed.

Brent began, "I was going through a really hard time in 2008. The stock market tanked, and I was in the middle of a very messy divorce. I texted you multiple times, and I never heard back. You basically ghosted me. The story I'm telling myself is that you didn't care about me, and you were only concerned with yourself. It made me feel sad, ashamed, and confused, and I couldn't understand why a good friend would turn his back on me. My role in this is that I shouldn't have let it fester for so long. I mean, it's been ten years, and I've never brought this up before. And what I want to know from you is what was going on."

"Brent, I'm really glad you brought this up," I replied. "Let me first play back what I'm hearing. You were going through a bad divorce in 2008. You needed me, and you felt that I turned my back on you. I'm so glad were talking about this because when I heard what you said, it made me feel sad and abandoned and embarrassed. I started my business at the end of 2007, and I distinctly remember getting those texts and thinking, 'How can I deal with this right now when I'm running out of cash, trying to hire people, dealing with potential patent infringement and the stresses of starting a new company?' I was working sixteen-hour days and had two little kids. All of that happened to coincide with the timing of your divorce. And I apologize for that. I should have recognized the strain in the relationship and tried to figure this out sooner. I didn't realize how much this hurt you and how long you were holding onto this."

"Oh, my gosh," Brent exclaimed. "I had no idea that all of that was going on at the same time. It totally makes sense now."

And with that, we both agreed that we were clear. I was grateful we had the conversation, but also sad we hadn't had it ten years earlier. We could have avoided a decade of built-up resentment.

Much like having a pebble stuck in your shoe when you are on a run or a long hike, you want to clear issues as they arise. Take care of small issues, so they don't become big ones. The clearing model is a way to protect your relationships and restore balance before that happens.

In the words of Don Miguel Ruiz in *The Four Agreements:* "All human problems would be resolved if we could just have good, clear communication."

## GETTING TO THE MAGIC

Ultimately, people want to be seen and known, but building deep relationships is easier for some than for others. Connecting with people is an art. The good news is you can get better at it.

When I am on a BusinessOutside hike with corporate executives —one-on-one or in a facilitated group setting—I like to go a little deeper, beyond superficial small talk. I think about it like a bell curve. I call it the *Nature of Conversations*. Let's say that small talk and other surface-level conversations take up 70 percent of our day-to-day interactions at work, in public, and even at home. At the trailhead, I may start by drawing a bell curve in the dirt.

It's the 10 percent of conversations on each side of the bell curve where conversations dip a little deeper and touch on some real emotion. Beyond that, there's 5 percent that you rarely talk to anybody about—the intimate revelations you would typically reserve only for really close friends or family members. This is where I like to build the foundation of all my relationships and interactions. In fact, I try to get somewhere within the 5 or 10 percent the first time I meet people. The best way I know to do that is to be the first to share, be vulnerable, and to share beyond day-to-day surface-level interactions.

Of course, these kinds of deeper conversations don't happen right away. I might start by sharing some surface-level information about myself:

"Life's pretty good. I have two kids, sixteen and eighteen. I live in Boulder, Colorado. I'm a consultant facilitator and executive coach, and I like public speaking. I moved here from Atlanta seven years ago. I like to hike. I love the outdoors. I love open water swimming. I like connecting with people."

All of that is superficial, right in the middle of the 70 percent. Then I would point to the 10 percent of the bell curve and share something more personal:

"My daughter is eighteen, and she's a great kid. She's a good student. I am so lucky, but I feel like she's gone. I have a really flexible schedule and I'm able to be at home, but I hardly ever see her. She will come home from school, drop her backpack, and say, 'Hey, Dad, I'm heading to the gym.' Immediately she takes off to be with friends (or to do whatever teenagers do with their time). I realize she is ready to go to college and a chapter of my life is ending. And it makes me sad because I feel like she's already left."

At this point I start hiking again. I find that physical movement allows the conversation to continue to flow. This is a big advantage of doing business outside.

I might go on to say I founded a business in healthcare technology that put health kiosks that screen for blood pressure and vision in places like Walmart and Safeway. I might explain, "In the summer of 2012, I got a phone call from Walmart I had been waiting four years for. That call changed everything. They said our pilot had exceeded their expectations and asked how soon we could get health kiosks into four thousand stores. Our business took off like a rocket. We ended up raising $50 million in capital, and in the summer of 2012, we deployed 2,500 units over three months. We were producing fifty a day, installing forty a day, and hiring like crazy. It was all so exciting."

Sharing some details about my business can help others—especially other business owners and entrepreneurs—feel more comfortable. They understand the challenges I've faced. But I don't stop there. I ultimately want to shift to the 5 percent, which requires real vulnerability. At this point I aim to step out of my comfort zone and share something I don't typically share with people. I might say: "I earned a very valuable lesson along the way. When you raise $50 million in capital, it's not your company anymore. I ended up being forced out of the company I founded. I was embarrassed, hurt, and angry. Who was I without the CEO title? I had no idea what I was going to do next."

By sharing in this way, I invite the other person into a space of vulnerability. Over and over again, I've seen others listen to what I have to share and say something like, "I'm so glad you shared. Let me tell you what's happened to me." We move right into the 10 percent, and that begins a real relationship grounded in authenticity —in which we can share failures, show imperfections, admit to insecurities, and be real.

Vulnerability is the point of connection that opens the door for trust, authentic communication, and deep relationships. Every time I open up, I can see the change in someone's demeanor—in their eyes, and in their facial expression. If we are hiking, they may stop briefly and look at me. It's that moment when I realize I have made a personal connection.

Sometimes it's necessary to intentionally make the shift from small talk to meaningful conversation even with people we're already connected to. I often have to do this with a really good friend I've known for thirty years. The first five minutes of our conversations are usually filled with idle talk over a beer about our favorite sports teams. We go through this monotony of small talk because it's what we've always done. But at some point, one of us will ask, "Well, how's it *really* going? How is work *really*?" Or I'll start moving things in a different direction by sharing something I'm struggling with or losing sleep over. My voice softens, and the speed of the conversation changes. He might turn the TV down or say something like, "Hold on. I want to step outside for privacy."

*Those* are the conversations I love because that's where the magic happens: the rich conversations where an emotional connection is shared. And when we learn how someone is truly feeling, it's much easier to have genuine empathy for them. Often we think everyone else has their life together and that we're alone in our pain and insecurities. Being vulnerable allows the other person to feel safe and to share openly, and ultimately allows us to know we're not alone.

It definitely takes more energy to stay in that 5 and 10 percent of conversations. It is a lot easier to have a superficial conversation about the weather, your job, or game seven. Getting to the emotion and the feelings tied to whatever you are sharing—that's where the deeper connections happen.

In our society, we often feel we need to look "the part" and put on a metaphorical mask for protection. We live in the Instagram age where people post unrealistic perfect images of their life. It's easy to feel alone in it all. When we share, we give each other permission to not be perfect, and not have it all figured out. These types of conversations facilitate the kind of connection that allows for that 2:00 a.m. phone call.

Here's what I hope you remember: Vulnerability isn't a weakness. It's a superpower. Embracing vulnerability will have profound impacts on your personal and professional lives. And it can inspire a new, more open, authentic, and healthy culture in your business.

## Building a Personal Board of Directors

In my YPO forum, a global leadership community of successful chief executives, I feel like I can share without holding anything back and receive unvarnished advice, guidance, and input in return. People genuinely care about me as a human, which is sometimes more difficult to find at work because each company has its own hierarchy and chain of command. At the C-suite level, there are not many people you can talk to without reservation. For me, having a group like YPO has meant so much because I can be authentic with the knowledge that everyone there has my best interests at heart.

Beyond YPO, I've adopted a few strong mentors, essentially creating a personal board of directors. Tom Lamb, the former COO of Lexmark Permian, has been one of my advisors since he became an early investor in SoloHealth. He likes to say he is a "boat tapper." The boat is going down the river, but every once in a while, it gets a little bit off course. He comes in to tap the back of the boat.

We all need a boat tapper. You are doing everything else—paddling, steering, navigating—but the boat tapper helps you stay on course. Having one or more boat tappers in your life will always be helpful. The more you can surround yourself with champions who are looking out for you, the happier and more successful you will be.

In turn, you are offering these connections part of yourself and an opportunity for them to contribute to you. *That* is connection.

## Start Small, Then Build

Building relationships is a lot like building a campfire: it's important to start with tinder. Using small logs and dry firewood is the most effective way to get that fire going. Once the fire is burning strongly, you can throw pretty much anything on top—even wet logs—and it's going to continue burning. The mistake some people make is trying to start that fire with lighter fluid and paper. It may get a quick spark and look great momentarily, but it burns out quickly. If you want to cultivate quality relationships, you have to be patient, start in small increments, and build to a roaring flame.

Cultivating relationships without asking for anything in return is only the beginning—the tinder you use to build the long-burning heat source. What really matters is the deeper level connections and establishing rapport. In the end, you will have all the support you need—a few select boat tappers and an entire cheering squad with a vested interest in your success—and these people will get you further, faster.

You do not have to build your business, or your life, alone. These deep relationships and longtime friends are a strong, solid foundation, like the firewood that keeps the fire raging strongly.

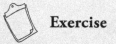 **Exercise**

Make a list of five people who inspire you and give you energy. Now determine what meaningful steps you can take to spend more time with these people. Write them down and take that first step. Start small, then build.

# CHAPTER FOUR

# Personal Values Statement

*"Values are like fingerprints. Nobody's are the same,
but you leave them all over everything you do."*

—ELVIS PRESLEY

I REMEMBER MY DAD SITTING ME DOWN WHEN I WAS NINE OR TEN years old and saying, "You know, son, if you work for yourself, you have the flexibility to set your own schedule, be your own boss, and have more freedom." His words resonated with me. I understood then that I needed to be intentional and set the direction of my own life. I also understood that if I worked for someone else, I was just fulfilling their dream instead of my own. It made sense, then, when I pinpointed *personal freedom* as my top personal value.

I discovered a personal values exercise from a good friend and YPO Forum mate, Christy Orris, who runs a nonprofit called Peak to Peak Leadership with her husband, Jay. It has made a big impact on me and my life because it helped me craft my own personal values statement, which became my North Star and guides me in my decision-making for all aspects of my life. Now I teach this process to others to help them discover their personal values. Getting clarity on your personal values is foundational. Knowing what you truly value provides direction, inspiration, and guidance in the course of your life.

## WHAT ARE YOUR VALUES?

When I teach values in a workshop, I first ask, "What are values and why are they important?"

Typically, the responses will be things like, "They're my moral compass," or "They help ground me." Others might view values as a guidepost or lodestar. All of those answers are right. You can define this term how you want, as long as you are clear why values matter to you.

### Values Exercise

The personal values exercise helps you identify what is most important in your life. It also provides a good tool to use with your team. Once others know your personal values, and you know theirs, you can better understand their motivations. You will become more aware of what gives you energy and where you spend your time.

To do this exercise, you will use a personal values sheet.

You can find this sheet at www.BusinessOutside.com/Values or in the Appendix in the back of this book. Included are forty-six different values, such as love, family, and loyalty. Take a moment to scan the list.

1. Look at all the values in the list and locate the importance of each value to you by placing a check next to:

   a. Not Important

   b. Slightly Important

   c. Really Important

2. Look through the values you have marked as really important and choose the ten most important values and add a check for them in the TOP 10 column. If you feel there are any important values missing, write them in the spaces at the bottom.

3. Choose the five most important values from the Top 10. Put a check in the TOP 5 Column. Now pick the values you want in the TOP 3 Column. These are your core values.

4. Finally, from your three core values, choose your NUMBER 1, most important value.

I've had groups ask if the values they are choosing should represent who they are today—in this moment—or if these values should be more aspirational. I never give guidance because I want the person doing the exercise to choose.

For the purpose of this book, I encourage you to do this exercise two times: the first, choosing values that represent who you are and where you are in this moment; and the second, locating your aspirational values, keeping in mind that your values evolve as your circumstances evolve. Maybe today your values align with ambition and goal setting, but later in life you hope your values will be more about personal freedom. Try it both ways, and see what you come up with.

## Crafting Your Personal Values Statement

You can use the top words that resonate to create a personal values statement. This statement is important because it helps you clarify what you truly value in life in just a few lines. When you combine this statement with your Zone of Genius, which we'll discuss in the next chapter, you'll have a North Star, a guide for making decisions.

The following is my personal values statement, which I created by following the steps I've outlined here.

> I value **personal freedom**, which allows me to lead an **active** and **healthy** life full of **adventure**. I will build **authentic** and **loving relationships** with **friends** and **family**. I will fulfill myself through **curiosity**, **personal growth**, and **lifelong learning**.

Here are a few other examples of personal values statements from people who have attended my workshops:

"My health and family define what is most important in my life. These ground me and motivate me. When I focus on these values, I experience peace, lead with integrity, and strive for excellence in all I do in life."

"I live my life with integrity at all times. I value relationships with family and the importance of friendship. Loyalty to those I care about the most is paramount to painting a palace of physical health and self-respect."

"My family is my most important responsibility. I seek to build strong personal friendships, personally and professionally. I strive to keep an open mind and maintain the courage to continually pursue personal growth. I ensure I approach all that I do with the highest integrity."

"I act with integrity in everything I do. My relationships with friends and family are built on trust. These key relationships nurture my personal growth and empower me to focus on my physical and mental health."

These lead-in prompts can help you begin to craft this statement for yourself:

I act...
I believe...
I value...
I will fulfill myself by...
I will build...
Pursuing...

When working with groups, I will ask the participants to take out a piece of paper to write their personal values statement. I tell them that what I'm looking for is their "SFD." I write it in large, block lettering on the whiteboard. SFD stands for "shitty first draft." This concept was originated by Anne Lamott in her popular book about writing, *Bird by Bird*. She argues for the need to let go and write those "shitty first drafts" that lead to clarity and sometimes brilliance in our second and third drafts.

It is the same when crafting your personal values statement. I want people to realize that it doesn't have to be perfect. It is a work in progress. But once you feel you have nailed your personal values statement, it becomes a compass. When you are faced with a challenge or opportunity, you will know what to do.

I remember when I was asked to join as president of a large division of a publicly traded health and wellness company. As I was trying to decide whether to accept or decline the offer, I looked at my personal values statement, specifically my top value: *personal freedom.* How would that tie in with a job that required me to be in the office all day, every day 8:00 a.m. to 5:00 p.m., Monday through Friday? It seemed clear that the offer was in conflict with my top value. And how would this position lead to an active and healthy lifestyle? The opportunity would fulfill *some* of my values—but, man, it sure did not hit those most important to me. My values statement helped me ultimately realize that I couldn't accept the position. I knew the job would be a much better fit for someone who lists financial security or stability as their top values.

By using this exercise in practice, my values became more real. This deeper understanding of myself was like an *aha* moment for me.

## Sharing Your Statement with Others

The final step of this exercise is to share it with others—family, coworkers, or friends. Once you know someone else's personal values—particularly those of a coworker or a loved one—it helps you understand how they think. I did this exercise with Aly. As I looked at her list, I said, "That's really strange. Only two of your values are the same as mine."

Right away, she said, "Oh, family and health."

"How did you know that?" I asked, since Aly hadn't seen my values statement yet.

"Oh, because you don't care about this other stuff," she answered casually.

I laughed. Aly really understands me.


## Benefits of Understanding Others' Personal Values

Understanding another person's personal values can offer insight into how to interact with them. You will have a better understanding of how a person is likely to react to a comment or situation, or how a concept will land with them, if you know their personal values.

Knowing Aly's top personal values helps me reframe certain conversations so that she is able to receive them more openly. For her, trust is not aspirational, but a primary way of being. Our marriage works because Aly fully trusts me in my role as financial provider, which allows her to feel stable and safe in her role as family CEO. On the other hand, she knows my top values and honors the flexibility and freedom I need to live out my purpose.

Although it is often helpful when we share values in common with the people we love and work with, it can be equally beneficial to have different ones. If Aly and I shared the same top values—if personal freedom and adventure were also top priorities for her—our marriage wouldn't work as well.

Knowing each other's personal values can also open a conduit for resolution, especially when there's conflict. When you experience conflict, you can now ask: *what sort of solutions will work for both party's personal values?*

We tend to best understand people who share similar values. We want to be around them because they inspire us to be the best versions of ourselves. They exhibit the values we aspire to, and give us an example of what the values look like in action. However, surrounding yourself with people with different values keeps life interesting. People who move through life differently than we do can provide a unique perspective, challenge our beliefs, and help us expand our thinking.

## Respecting People's Values

When somebody challenges or embraces one of your personal values, how does it make you feel?

In my marriage, I've learned how important it is to embrace someone's personal values. By embracing Aly's values in our everyday life, I show her that I understand what is important to her and am not doubting her value statement. For example, I've learned over the years how important *trust* is for Aly. So, if I notice that our cable bill looks a little high and ask Aly to call the cable company to figure out why, I know I shouldn't then start questioning her when I return home.

If she tells me she called and they couldn't do anything, I can't start micromanaging her, or insinuating that I could have done it better. If I did, her response would be, "Do you not trust that I am competent enough to handle this?"

When somebody challenges our personal values, we tend to have a strong reaction. These reactions are not always rational; they are emotional because the challenge can feel like an attack on our character, what we believe, and who we are. Still, if you know someone else's personal values, it's important to believe them and not continually challenge them to prove that they hold those values.

## Values Assessment and Alignment

While it's important not to question what others say they value, it can be useful to turn that question inward to challenge yourself. How much does your life reflect your personal values? If you put family as your top personal value, but you are working ten to twelve hours a day, you have an opportunity for reflection. You can tell yourself that you work so much so you can provide for your family, but if you seldom spend any time with them, your values and life are out of alignment.

To help you identify these inconsistencies and bring your values and your day-to-day life into better alignment, you can use the final piece in the values exercise: the values assessment.

1. Review and write out your top five values.

2. Ask yourself, on a scale of one to five (one is "Never" and five is "Always"), how much have you been leaning into this value over the last year? How about in the last three to six months? In other words, how much has your behavior been aligned with your values? Put the number one to five next to each value so you can see the alignment or lack of alignment visually.

3. Identify the top values that you're not currently practicing at a five. How can these values become more consistent in your life? Ask yourself what you need to do to move the needle in the right direction. You will have to be completely honest with yourself to make any real change.

## Memorable Moments Can Help You

I use the 1 Second Everyday video app to capture memorable moments. The app allows you to record one second of video every day, and then it chronologically edits or mashes them together in a single film. When I am at my happiest, my second for that day reflects my top personal values. If you are in transition or you can't articulate what has value in your life, this 1 Second Everyday app may help you gain clarity.

If I were to watch my videos over the last three months, six months, or year, most of those videos would illustrate what I value the most: my personal freedom, an active and healthy lifestyle, authentic relationships, time with family, curiosity, outdoor adventure, growth, and lifelong learning. It's all there.

Try out this app or a similar method for capturing memorable moments. Then take the opportunity to ask yourself, How much does my life reflect my personal values statement? This is a quick way to accurately answer that question. And then, if necessary, to course-correct.

I'm willing to bet that at least one area of your life doesn't reflect your personal values at all. Maybe you value health, but you're not scheduling time to exercise. Maybe you value friendship or personal connection but rarely see the friends who mean the most to you. Perhaps you really value fun and laughter, yet your whole day feels like a grind, from the minute you get up to the minute you go to bed and you can't remember the last time you had a good belly laugh.

Of course, you want to feel personal fulfillment in your career, but if a core value is fun and you don't have that, look at how you can start incorporating more fun, play, and laughter into your life. You don't have to make a dramatic change. Simply determine what fun looks like for you and take a step toward alignment. For example, you could commit to a date night with your spouse, or having the guys over to watch football, or a weekly round of golf.

Now that you know your personal values, you can use them to ensure your life does not happen *to* you but is created *by* you. You can serve as an inspirational example to those around you, including your coworkers and employees. You can take yet another step towards building a BusinessOutside culture.

# CHAPTER FIVE

# Zone of Genius

> *"You are unique. You have different talents and abilities.*
> *You don't have to always follow in the footsteps of others.*
> *And most important, you should always remind yourself that*
> *you don't have to do what everyone else is doing and have a*
> *responsibility to develop the talents you have been given."*
>
> —ROY T. BENNETT

WHEN I WAS IN HIGH SCHOOL, I WANTED TO BECOME AN ORTHO-pedic surgeon. I liked sports and knew this career would allow me to work with athletes. Plus, I had read that orthopedic surgeons make a lot of money. The job seemed like a great fit, or so I thought.

In my sophomore year, I signed up for Advanced Placement (AP) biology. The teacher for that class had been voted Teacher of the Year for the state of Florida. His class was popular, but I got in. The first day, he reviewed the syllabus and told us the first week was going to be easy because it would be a review of the previous year.

That sounded great until I realized I was already lost with the "review content." I had no idea what the teacher was talking about. "Next week," he said, "we will start getting into the real meat." I panicked.

My mom encouraged me to see the guidance counselor, so I did. I told her the review material was over my head, and I didn't know what to do. Very matter-of-factly, she said, "Well, okay, let's pull you out of AP biology. We'll just put you in the normal biology class." At the time, this felt like a devastating solution to my problem. I wanted to become an orthopedic surgeon, and this move certainly wouldn't support the dream. I told the guidance counselor as much.

"Bart, listen," she said. "This might be hard to hear, but to be an orthopedic surgeon you have to be really, really good at science—and you're not. You also have to be really good at math. Are you good at math?"

"No," I said, feeling dejected.

"Well, that's okay. You can go in a different direction."

For her, it was all very simple. But to me, this news came as a major letdown. *What was I going to do with my life now?* The guidance counselor must have seen the confusion on my face.

"Bart, you're seventeen," she said with a little laugh, "You can do anything. But you have to focus on something you're really passionate about, and are great at."

Before that conversation, no one had ever asked me if I liked science or math. I had never realized how much I disliked those subjects or how challenging they would be until that AP biology class. Up to that point, there was only one route available. Now I began to wonder how true that was. Why couldn't I pursue work that aligned to who I was by nature? This conversation was a wake-up call; it showed me the importance of finding my *Zone of Genius* and set me on a new path of discovery.

The first step on this new path was to focus on what I loved and was great at. I didn't know it at the time, but my guidance counselor was pointing to a concept later coined by Dan Sullivan in his book, *Unique Ability.* He uses that phrase to describe a powerful force that is at the very core of who a person is as an individual.

A few years later, psychologist Gay Hendricks coined the term "Zone of Genius" to refer to the times when a person is working from their innate abilities. No matter what you call it, this is the state in which you find ceaseless inspiration, may lose track of time, and create distinguished work that excels beyond what anyone else is doing.

In this chapter, you will learn how to identify and harness your own Zone of Genius.

## IDENTIFYING YOUR ZONE OF GENIUS

In *Unique Ability*, Dan Sullivan teaches a discovery process that helps people find their Zone of Genius (even though he didn't call it that). He starts by advising you to email ten of your closest friends and colleagues and ask them where they think you excel. With those answers in hand, you can then determine whether these points of excellence are also things you truly love doing. You might be talented in many ways, but there's certainly no reason to spend all your time doing things that don't bring you joy.

Hendricks offers additional insight on how to find your Zone of Genius in *The Big Leap: Conquer Your Hidden Fear and Take Life to the Next Level*. He poses the following "genius questions":

- *What do I most love to do?* (I love it so much I can do it for long stretches of time without getting tired or bored.)
- *What work do I do that doesn't seem like work?* (I can do it all day long without ever feeling tired or bored.)
- *In my work, what produces the highest ratio of abundance and satisfaction to the amount of time spent?* (Even if I do only ten seconds or a few minutes of it, an idea or a deeper connection may spring forth that leads to huge value.)
- *What is my unique ability?* (There's a special skill I'm gifted with. This unique ability, fully realized and put to work, can provide enormous benefits to me and any organization I serve.)

Some of these questions are professionally oriented, but you can think about how they relate to all areas of your life, including volunteer work, hobbies, and parenting. You can also write out ideas in stream of consciousness using phrases like:

I'm at my best when I'm _____.
When I'm at my best, the exact thing I'm doing is _____.
When I'm doing that, the thing I love most about it is _____.

Conversely, you can look at what falls *outside* your Zone of Genius by asking questions like:

- What zaps my energy?
- What do I avoid doing?
- What produces the least abundance and satisfaction for the time spent?

It's important to be conscious of what falls outside your Zone of Genius so you're not spinning your wheels trying to do things you shouldn't be doing. After all, others can fulfill these spaces much better because they have their own unique Zones of Genius. It does no one any good to try to be something or someone you're not.

A simple formula you can use to identify your Zone of Genius is to identify the intersection of your talent *and* your passion. Note that passion goes beyond things you *like*; we all like a lot of things. Instead, you want to identify the things that get you out of bed in the morning, give you energy, and make you feel like you are uniquely positioned to deliver this service to the world. You can use a simple chart like the following:

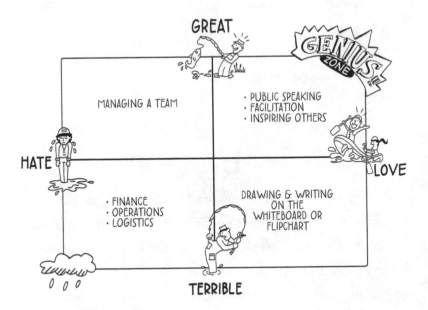

When I learned this formula, I found that my Zone of Genius was clear and apparent. I can set a vision and get people excited. That's what I love to do, and it has manifested into facilitating events and speaking. Once I discovered my personal values and combined them with my Zone of Genius, things really started clicking.

Now, complete this chart for yourself:

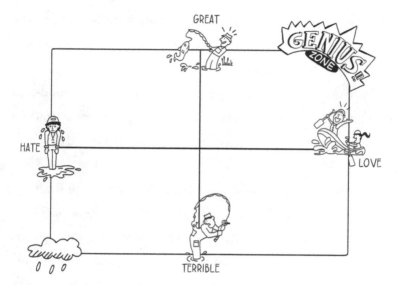

## Moral Responsibility

It's amazing to see well-known athletes, celebrities, and CEOs operating in their Zones of Genius, but all of us have access to our own Zone of Genius. And when we find it, not only will we be able to operate with greater ease and efficiency, but we will be of greater service to the world. At the same time, we'll be able to recognize others living in their Zones of Genius and look to them for specific jobs. In this way, we fulfill a moral responsibility in two ways: we honor both ourselves and others.

Mark Manson, a self-help author and blogger, co-authored Will Smith's book, *Will*. Manson wrote on his website that some of the most important insights he gained from Will had to do with being a professional.[12] For example, Will once told Manson, "I'm world-class at only a couple of things. And every hour I'm not doing those things, I am doing a disservice to myself and the world."

He continued, "There are people out there who are world-class at other things—cooking, marketing, writing, whatever—and for me to *not* hire them and support what they do, also does a disservice to the world."

This same concept is reflected in business as well. In his landmark book, *Good to Great: Why Some Companies Make the Leap and Others Don't*, Jim Collins wrote: "We need to get everyone in the right seat on the bus." I've seen the importance of this simple idea firsthand. When you encourage your people to leverage their unique abilities, you not only create more efficiency but also produce better outcomes for the business.

Thinking of our Zones of Genius in ethical terms might be new, but doing so will change how you approach the idea in every sphere of life. *You have a moral responsibility to do what you do best, because that is your service to the world.* Similarly, you have a moral responsibility to support others in what *they* do best, because that is their service to the world.

---

[12] "An Indomitable Will," Mark Manson, June 21, 2021, https://markmanson.net/news letters/mindfck-monday-88?utm_campaign=mmnet-newsletter-06-21-2021&utm_medium =email&utm_source=mmnet-newsletter&utm_content=web-version.

## LIVING INTO YOUR ZONE OF GENIUS

Humans of New York (HONY) is an online photography project that was founded by Brandon Stanton in 2010. It features portraits and interviews conducted on the streets of New York. HONY now has more than twenty million followers and counting.

Stanton wasn't always a professional photographer. As a young man, he was a bond trader and planned to work in finance in order to save money and follow an artistic path later in life. But soon enough, he realized his job as a bond trader was stifling and didn't give him space to be creative.

When he lost his job, he bit the bullet and started practicing photography with zero training, but 100 percent passion. Stanton later reflected, "My two biggest lessons that I learned as a bond trader were taking risks and getting comfortable with taking losses and setbacks to help move you forward. Instead of updating my resume and looking for a similar job, I decided to forget about money and...have a go at something I truly loved."[13]

His photography led to interviewing the people whose photos he was taking. He discovered this was fulfilling and energizing, and it was tapping into something that he hadn't tapped into before. The work gave him a ton of energy and eventually became his full-time job.[14]

---

[13] Izzy Best, "How a Former Bond Trader Turned Photography into a Viral Hit," CNBC, December 6, 2014, https://www.cnbc.com/2014/12/05/how-ex-bond-traders-humans-of-new-york-became-a-viral-hit.html.

[14] Brandon Stanton, "Humans of New York: Behind the Lens," *Huffington Post*, May 3, 2013, https://www.huffpost.com/entry/humans-of-new-york-behind_b_3210673.

If you're feeling stuck or stifled, it may be time to start living into your Zone of Genius. You might not change your career right away, but taking steps in the right direction can certainly lead you down a whole new path. Sometimes the change happens fast, and sometimes it takes time.

Some of the most famous people in the world started the career they're known for late in life. Donald Fisher was forty years old and had no experience in retail when he and his wife, Doris, opened the first Gap store in San Francisco in 1969. Henry Ford was forty-five when he created the revolutionary Model T car in 1908. Vera Wang started out as a figure skater, before becoming a journalist. She didn't open her first bridal boutique until she was forty years old. Rodney Dangerfield is remembered as a legendary comedian, but he didn't catch a break until he made a hit appearance on *The Ed Sullivan Show* at age forty-six. Julia Child worked in advertising and media before writing her first cookbook when she was fifty, launching her career as a celebrity chef in 1961. Sam Walton had a fairly successful retail-management career in his twenties and thirties, but his path to astronomical success began at age forty-four, when he founded the first Walmart in Rogers, Arkansas, in 1962.

Clearly, all of these people needed some time to tap into their true Zones of Genius, but our lives are richer because they did. You might be able to only take one step in the right direction today, but that step could go a long way ten years from now.

Wherever you are, you don't have to feel trapped. Start by identifying what you really want to do, and then spend as much of your time as possible in your Zone of Genius. By taking daily steps, you can reach your potential, live out your personal values, and make the world a better place.

## Living Outside Your Zone of Genius

When someone is not working in their Zone of Genius, it is harder for them and others to see the missed opportunity. Perhaps they are an amazing graphic artist but rarely give their art time because of their busy job in inside sales. Maybe they're an amazing cook, but no one will know because they never share their gift with others. Other times opportunities get missed because a person doesn't share about their passion with others or feels blocked or trapped and is not able to see opportunities right in front of them.

HONY often features the stories of people who missed opportunities. One of the stories features Michael Saviello, who worked in a barbershop but was actually an extremely talented painter. As a child, his father sent him to Italy every summer. He would look at all of the famous paintings and think, "I could do this stuff." But he never pursued the craft in a real way. Instead, he went to business school at Rutgers, and right after graduation he got a job at a barbershop. He thought he would do it for a few weeks until he figured out something else. On his very first day, he saw people lined up outside the door. It was the hottest barbershop in town, and before he knew it, he was completely distracted by the busyness of the shop.

Thirty years passed by. Then, in 2016, a customer came into the barbershop and showed Saviello a book he wrote. Upon seeing this, Saviello said to himself, "That's it, this guy is a stockbroker, and he wrote a book. I'm going to start painting." (That stockbroker was Stanton, the founder of HONY.)

Every day during his lunch break, Saviello started going to the back room and painted for an hour. He was discovered and featured in a *New York Times* article entitled "The Michelangelo of the Barbershop" and eventually got his own solo show at a gallery.

Saviello explained that his entire life he had been saying, "I can do that." He always knew it. But he then finally did it. "So now other people know it, too."

Sometimes we don't have to change our job to start living in our Zone of Genius. Sometimes we simply need to change our language— the way we talk to ourselves. Instead of using words like, "I plan to," "I wish..." "I am going to..." "I should..." try out, "I commit..." You'll be amazed at how rapidly things can change. Saviello "committed" to painting one hour a day. He made it happen, and the rest is history.

## ZONE OF GENIUS AT WORK

In big companies, people often get saddled working on tasks that fall outside their Zone of Genius. This is especially true when you are working on a team, and there are so many things that have to get done. For example, let's say you're the marketing person. You feel it's your duty to do the fifteen tasks in your job description. The only problem is that you're not actually good at all those tasks. Maybe you're great at creating content for slides but are terrible with graphics. Well, it doesn't matter. The job description says you do the graphics, so you do the graphics.

If you agree with Will Smith that it is our responsibility to empower other people to focus on their genius, I'm sure you can see why it's so important to rethink this approach. As a team, how can we all plan our work around our respective Zones of Genius? I would take Jim Collins' "right seat, right bus" concept a step further. You could be in the right seat, but there might be just that one task that someone else is far better at.

An advisor in my firm BusinessOutside has a practice she does with her global team to encourage them to operate in their Zone of Genius. She has them create digital baseball cards, an idea she got from *New York Times* bestselling author of *Principles*, Ray Dalio. On the cards, they list their strengths, weaknesses, what gives them joy, what their ideal job would be, and other personal "stats." They then present their digital baseball cards to the team, and honest and powerful conversations bloom, resulting in more empathy, understanding, and happier teammates. And their productivity increases, too, as they work more from their strengths than weaknesses.

Whenever I have the opportunity to interview someone for a job, I like to ask: "If I invited a group of all of your former colleagues, bosses, and close friends to see a list all the tasks we need to get done in our growing company—influencing customers, managing financial controls, documenting processes, managing a team, having difficult conversations, and so forth—what are the three or four tasks that everyone in the room would agree you would be the best at? Conversely, what are the three or four tasks they would say you definitely shouldn't be doing?" By asking these simple questions, I begin to get a sense of the person's Zone of Genius and where they would be moving outside of that zone.

We owe it to ourselves, our colleagues, and our company to operate in our Zone of Genius as often as we can. If you're a business owner, you can support others to do this from as early as the interview stage, but after this open communication is necessary at every stage of the employee lifecycle. If someone on the team doesn't feel they can honestly share what works for them and what doesn't, there's no way to know who is living in their Zone of Genius and who is not.

## Monetizing Your Zone of Genius

Being both passionate and talented can be enough. But for practical reasons it also helps to ask: *can I make money with this skill?*

Sometimes, we can't answer that question right away, and that's okay. It took a full ten years of running HONY before Brandon Stanton began online fundraisers for some of the people he was profiling. Through his storytelling, he was able to lead record-breaking fundraisers: he helped a single mom named Esther who was raising three girls raise $433,153; and Saroj Goyal, a widow with breast cancer, raised $498,572. He helped raise a total of $2,697,720 for Stephanie, also known as Tanqueray, who was down on her luck, having health concerns, and about to be evicted from her home. Over time, Stanton became influential by being in service to other people, and telling their stories.

Stanton does not view this as charity. All his subjects bring a priceless resource to the table—their story. "We're just going to tell that story using a new model," Stanton says. "Instead of selling advertising, or selling it to a publisher, we're asking for voluntary contributions from anyone who's gotten value from these narratives. If the story of their lives has made you laugh, or cry, or think—please consider compensating the person who lived it. Because right now their story is the one thing they have to offer."

Because of his service to the community, Stanton was included in *Time* magazine's list of 30 people under 30 who are changing the world. Stanton was able to monetize this endeavor using Patreon, a membership platform that allows content creators to run a subscription service. It helps creators and artists earn a monthly income by providing rewards and perks to their subscribers.

Once you have a clearer idea of what your Zone of Genius is, you can start making small shifts toward spending more time in this zone without necessarily making immediate and drastic changes in your life. That being said, the goal is ultimately to spend the majority of your time living in this zone. By doing so, your relationships will evolve and your life will improve. To reach this goal, you will need to consider how you can monetize your Zone of Genius most effectively. Think outside the box whenever possible and take the next step, like Stanton did.

## Shaking the Tree

Years after the doomed AP biology class, I ran into Linda Anderson, my guidance counselor in my hometown. I told her that she helped change my life, and she cried.

When I tell the story of our conversation, some people react negatively, as if the counselor shouldn't have told me not to pursue my dreams, as if she somehow crushed my spirit. But, no, she saved me. She *shook the tree* and helped me see what needed to fall to the ground.

I wasn't good in math or science, and the content didn't excite me, yet I was about to pursue thirteen years of grueling math- and science-related education. It seems really harsh, but Mrs. Anderson spared me from struggling through four years of college, four years of medical school, and a five-year residency—during which time I would have inevitably come to the same conclusion. She saved me years of wasted time, energy, and money. She practiced kind candor, and we need more of that.

I'm also grateful that the signs were clear for me. Had I been pretty good at math and science, I might have gotten all the way into pre-med before having the awful realization that I was in the wrong place, pursuing something that didn't truly give me life.

Knowing what I know now about my Zone of Genius and my core value of personal freedom, I know I would have been miserable as an orthopedic surgeon. I can't imagine being permanently on-call, indoors, under fluorescent lights constantly, dealing with people's physical challenges. For someone who loves the structure, financial security, the ability to improve the quality of someone else's life by eradicating pain and setting them on a path to a healthier and happier life, this is an excellent career choice. But it's not for me, and it never was.

Perhaps you need to acknowledge a similarly hard truth. Or maybe you're living in your Zone of Genius only a small percentage of the time. Wherever you find yourself, it's time to get honest with yourself. Use the following question to quickly identify where you are.

**Self-Assessment:** On a scale of one to five, how well have I leaned into my Zone of Genius in the last three to six months?

Before you move on to the next chapters, be sure to take the time you need to solidify both your personal values statement and your Zone of Genius. These create a strong foundation from which the rest of your life can flow. And they are keys to doing BusinessOutside.

# CHAPTER SIX

# Energy Management

> *"Every day we awake with a certain amount of mental, emotional and physical energy that we spend throughout the day. If we allow our emotions to deplete our energy, we have no energy to change our lives or to give to others."*
>
> —DON MIGUEL RUIZ

THE MOST CRITICAL RESOURCE WE HAVE AS HUMAN BEINGS IS OUR energy.

There are four types of energy:

- ✓ Physical
- ✓ Emotional
- ✓ Mental
- ✓ Spiritual

It's normal to experience ebbs and flows in energy throughout life, but in order to live an intentional life and be our best selves *more of the time*, we need to align our energy investments with our purpose.

What I've realized over the years is that many of the executives and business leaders I work with manage their time well—hiring assistants to commandeer their calendars, outsourcing tasks, squeezing every last ounce out of their schedule—but those same leaders rarely know how to manage their energy.

Relying on grab-and-go food, rarely exercising, and spending almost no time outdoors during the week, many busy executives rarely even stop to take a drink of water. They are working long hours, staying on calls until they pull into the driveway, not giving themselves any time to decompress. With no separation between work and home, they get into the house and plop down on the couch, exhausted. They might grab a drink to help them unwind, and by the time their kids want them to read a book before bed, they are falling asleep. They *say* they value and cherish their family, but their actions demonstrate otherwise.

Clearly, something is out of alignment. Even if you are not an executive, you may still recognize some of these patterns. If any of this sounds like you, it's time to learn to manage your energy differently.

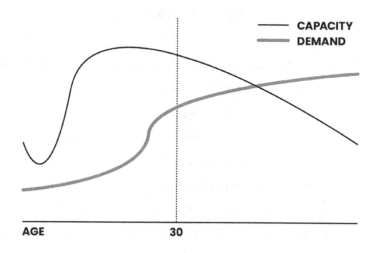

This graph shows our energy capacity versus our energy demand. As we grow older, demand overtakes capacity. After age thirty, our demand keeps increasing, but our capacity starts decreasing. Between ages thirty-five and forty, capacity and demand converge. If this is what we can expect, do we have any real control over how we manage our energy? Can we continue to grow while still retaining physical, emotional, mental, and spiritual energy? The answer is *yes*. We can increase our capacity when we better understand how energy works and then take necessary steps to manage it. Let's consider the different types of energy one by one.

# PHYSICAL ENERGY

It's fair to say that most entrepreneurs, executives, and business owners are not doing what they need to do to perform at peak levels. Given all the responsibility they have, they can learn a thing or two from what world-class athletes do to maintain their peak performance. To learn more about peak performance, I interviewed world-renowned strength and conditioning coach, Erin Carson. Erin is the co-owner and operator of RallySport, a training facility and health club in Boulder, Colorado. She provides strength training programs for endurance athletes who are seeking to perform at their very best. Her clients include world champions, triathletes, and Olympians, as well as everyday athletes seeking excellence.

## Better Metrics

In business, we are taught that if you can't measure it, you can't manage it. But we rarely ask whether or not we are using the right metric in the first place. Erin shared insight from her world: "As an elite athlete you can measure how fast you swim, how many watts per kilogram you output on the bicycle, and how fast you can run up a hill. Sometimes your metrics are really good, but you still don't win." Her point hit home. So often, business leaders seem to have all the right skills, resources, and money, but their company is still not successful. Why?

What Erin said next really struck a chord: "We have to look beyond these traditional metrics. In sports performance, what we look at more than anything now is recovery. The better rested my athletes are, the better they perform."

Of course, knowing how well you rest requires completely different metrics. This made me think about my sleep patterns. I can remember when I was in the midst of running SoloHealth, my sleep directly correlated to the amount of money we had in the bank. When we were flush with cash, I felt more relaxed and slept well. When we were almost out of money I was restless, worrying constantly.

Erin went on to say, "There used to be no number for measuring sleep. We had no way of measuring the quality of sleep, but as a coach, I needed a metric. Sleep trackers started allowing us to measure the sleep, but I didn't want to know that my athletes were in bed for ten hours. I wanted to know *the quality* of their sleep and how it affected their performance."

The good news is that sleep trackers have continued to evolve, offering intricate sensors that measure heart rate variability and more. We can now evaluate the quality of our rest, not just the quantity. She explained, "There are now many activity trackers on the market that can help you determine if your restless nights are affecting your performance during the day."

## Recovery is the Key to High Performance

Erin went on to discuss the importance of recovery. "The more rested my athletes are, the more they are going to meet their overall objectives. The better rested we are, the more prepared we are going to be for better outcomes."

This made me think about my own clients. As an executive coach, how could I measure their energy level throughout the day? Managing time is one thing, but we need to have energy for the things that matter most. Erin went on to share the concept of "Periodization." It's a term used in performance that involves adjusting variables during workouts to improve performance. It also involves adjusting the volume of training to constantly challenge the body. This is equivalent to changing your work throughout the day—both the type of work and the intensity. For example, you might be heads down creating a presentation to deliver to the board; it's an intense two-hour sprint. Then you change gears by asking a colleague to lunch to share their vacation plans for the year ahead. This mental reset allows your body and your mind to regroup.

As you use periodization, you will need to take even more time to recover. *You have to recover.* If you want to keep exceeding expectations (being able to crush it in your professional and personal lives), you can't take recovery lightly. When you invest in self-care, you will see more of those supercompensation weeks, not less. But you need to be willing to slow down and let your body get the rest it needs.

## Nature Dose

As Erin got me thinking more about metrics, I was thrilled to discover a company called NatureQuant that has taken data to develop algorithms that can measure how much nature is around you physically: the amount of rivers, lakes, trees, air quality. Their app, Nature Dose™, can measure how much time you are spending inside and how often you are in nature and provides you with a "leaf score."

The data demonstrates that 120 minutes of nature a week will make you healthier, happier, and more successful. This is less than twenty minutes a day. This doesn't seem like a lot until you look at the fact that in the US, the average person spends 93 percent of their time indoors.[15]

Many people never realize how much time they spend indoors, behind their desk, in front of a computer. Similar to tracking key performance indicators (KPIs) for our business, or tracking your steps

---

[15] Neil E. Klepeis, et al., "The National Human Activity Pattern Survey (NHAPS): A Resource Assessing Exposure to Environmental Pollutants," *Journal of Exposure Science & Environmental Epidemiology* 11, 231–252 (2001), https://www.nature.com/articles/7500165.

for health benefits, NatureDose provides a way for you to maximize the benefits of being outside in nature.

## Managing Expectations

A big part of managing your physical energy is managing expectations. It's important to know what is actually possible in terms of your physical capability. As Erin put it: "You can't win at the Olympics and five weeks later win again at world championships."

I know what she means. When I return from three days of intensive facilitation with high-powered CEOs, I leave it all on the field. I am mentally, emotionally, and physically exhausted. Now, I know that if I run an intensive forum retreat or strategic planning meeting for a Board of Directors, I know I need to have a day or two to recover in between. Otherwise, I will not be able to show up with my "A" game for the next objective.

Managing expectations means knowing what you need to do to perform well in all areas of life, not just at work. Erin surprised me when she said, "If I really want to have a great vacation, I need to rest the week before it starts. Most of us would think, I need to crush it hard before I go on vacation. Well, you are not going to be able to bring it twice. If your family is really important, recover a little the week *before* you leave. If you want to show up for your kids and get in the pool and throw your five-year-old around, you simply can't work eighteen-hour days the week leading into a holiday. Your kid is going to be in the pool asking you to come and play, and you are not going to have that ability."

Erin and I went on to discuss how so many people say they can't take this kind of rest, let alone find space to rest during a typical day. The truth is that most people won't take this time, especially executives who have no control over their schedules. Erin shared her recommendation: "If you are going to stay at work until 8:00 p.m., take two hours in the middle of the day—for some movement, a walk in the park, or a workout. Doing so will reset your physiology far more effectively than a lunch out or a cup of coffee."

In order to take Erin's advice, you'll need to get better at managing expectations with your team. You simply cannot be "on" all of the time. That will not benefit anyone. You will also need to manage your own expectations, especially when dealing with stressful situations.

## Tips to Renew Energy

Here are a few suggestions for incorporating recovery into your everyday life:

1. **Go to bed early and wake up early.** Night owls have a much more difficult time dealing with the demands of today's business world, because typically they still have to get up with the early birds and be in the office. They're often groggy and unfocused in the morning, possibly running off of caffeine and sugary snacks to keep up their energy. If you're part of this group, you will benefit by establishing new sleep rituals. You can begin to change your circadian rhythms through the following behavioral changes.

2. **Maintain a consistent bedtime and wake-up time.**
   As important as the number of hours you sleep is the
   consistency of the recovery wave you create. Regular sleep
   cycles help regulate your other biological clocks and
   increase the likelihood that the sleep you get will be
   deep and restful.

3. **Seek recovery every 90 to 120 minutes.** Chronobiologists
   have found that the body's hormone, glucose, and blood
   pressure levels drop every ninety minutes or so. By failing
   to seek recovery and overriding the body's natural stress-rest
   cycles, overall capacity is compromised. As we've learned
   from athletes, even short, focused breaks can promote
   significant recovery. Erin suggests five sources of resto-
   ration: eat something, hydrate, move physically, change
   your mental and emotional state.

4. **Cut-back on those nightcaps and alcohol consumption.**
   Alcohol can wreck your sleep. Thanks to science, we're
   learning so much about how alcohol negatively impacts our
   mental and physical health, even in moderate amounts.
   So instead of reaching for that nightcap, reach for a book
   or chamomile tea. Perhaps save your nightcaps for the
   weekend or ditch them all together. An advisor on my
   team stopped drinking completely and says it unleashed
   "superpowers" for better sleep, productivity, and mental
   and physical energy. The benefits were so great she says,
   "I don't miss it one bit."

5. **Get outside.** One of the best things you can do for physical energy is get up early and go for a walk, hike, or a run outside. Find times to go outside and breathe in fresh air. As John Muir famously said, "I only went out for a walk and finally concluded to stay out till sundown, for going out, I found, was really going in." We all have the same amount of time. The difference is what we choose to do with it. We can all prioritize our physical health if we make it a priority.

You don't have to ignore your family so you can go to the gym. You can find a way to work movement into your day. Erin noted that for many people, twenty minutes of high-intensity exercise is enough.

As I shared earlier in the book, my approach is life integration. Why not take your family and coworkers with you so you can all be active together? By incorporating the outdoors and exercise into your life, you will stay healthy and have more energy without having to think so much about your physical well-being as a separate part of life.

Physical self-care is nonnegotiable, but we can't stop there. Let's take a look now at how we can manage our emotional energy.

## EMOTIONAL ENERGY

Emotions are energy in motion propelled by your thoughts. Positive emotions can fuel our performance, connection to others, and well-being. Some performance- and happiness-optimizing emotions are:

hope, gratitude, compassion, realistic optimism, a sense of adventure, kindness, and joy. These are the emotions we want to work on cultivating.

The old adage you are what you think is rooted in truth. The field of cognitive behavioral psychology and other similar fields have proven that many negative emotional states stem from faulty, unhealthy thinking, often derived from learned patterns of unhealthy thinking. By paying attention to our thoughts, and learning better, more healthy and positive ways of thinking, we can literally change our emotions.

The idea that our thoughts are foundational to how we feel and who we become isn't new. Ancient philosophers have been preaching this for centuries. The great Chinese philosopher and writer Lao Tzu said it this way: "Watch your thoughts, they become your words; watch your words, they become your actions; watch your actions, they become your habits; watch your habits, they become your character; watch your character, it becomes your destiny."

Close relationships are another powerful, essential means for promoting positive emotions and effective recovery. Anyone who has enjoyed a happy family reunion or an evening with good friends knows the profound sense of safety and security that these relationships can induce. Unfortunately, many corporate executives feel that in order to perform up to expectations at work, they have no choice but to sacrifice their time with their family. I believe it's important to reframe this idea. By devoting more time to your most important relationships and setting clear boundaries between work and home, you will not only derive more satisfaction but will also get the recovery you need to perform better at work.

**Emotional Energy Tips**

Each of the following resets your emotional energy and provides more clarity and focus:

→ Pay attention to your thinking. Don't dwell on negative, faulty thoughts.

→ Practice having an attitude of gratitude. Reflect on three things you are grateful for every day.

→ Breathe deeply for one minute. Try short meditative practices. (More on that below.)

→ Engage in physical activity, especially outdoors. It increases positive brain function.

→ Connect with people you love and respect. Healthy relationships fuel better emotional states.

## MENTAL ENERGY

Mental energy is the source of our ideas and thinking. There are many ways to power positive mental energy. Being outside provides a huge boost, but so does an engaging book, podcast, intriguing conversation, or any type of continuous learning.

What's especially helpful about the outdoors is that there are no digital distractions. No computer. No phone. When you're walking or hiking, you can be more mindful and intentional with your thoughts, which can in turn boost mental energy. Anything that interferes with focus dissipates energy.

Mental and emotional states overlap and intertwine, each helping fuel the other. For example, meditation is an excellent practice for both your mental and emotional energy. Meditation, typically viewed as a spiritual practice, can serve as a highly practical means of training attention and promoting recovery. At a basic level, no guidance from a guru is required. A perfectly adequate meditation technique is to sit quietly and breathe deeply. Count each exhalation for ten seconds, inhale for ten seconds, and then start over. Alternatively, you can choose a word to repeat each time you take a breath.

Practiced regularly, meditation quiets the mind, the emotions, and the body, promoting energy recovery. Numerous studies have shown, for example, that experienced meditators need considerably fewer hours of sleep than non-meditators.[16] Meditation and other non-cognitive disciplines can also slow brain wave activity and stimulate a shift in mental activity from the left hemisphere of the brain to the right.[17] Have you ever found the solution to something that has been bothering you while you are doing something completely mindless, like running, gardening, or swimming? That's the left brain, right brain shift at work.

---

[16] Prachant Kaul, Jason Passafiume, Craig R. Sargent, Bruce F. O'Hara, "Meditation Acutely Improves Psychomotor Vigilance, and May Decrease Sleep Need," *Behavioral and Brain Functions* (2010) 6: 47, https://www.ncbi.nlm.nih.gov/pmc/articles/PMC2919439/.

[17] "Do You Need Less Sleep When You Meditate?" Long Island Spine Specialist, accessed March 19, 2022, https://www.lispine.com/blog/do-you-need-less-sleep-when-you-meditate/.

Learning new things and challenging your mind is another way to strengthen your mental energy. And these also help with maintaining a growth mindset. I challenge myself to learn something new every day—and to tackle a bigger mental challenge at least once a month.

This isn't as daunting as it may seem. There are many "learning hacks" to spur your mental energy. Listening to podcasts and other audio is an incredibly efficient and enjoyable way to learn. You can listen while exercising, in the car running errands, or washing the dishes. Online learning and educational platforms also provide a ton of engaging opportunities. Our digital world offers unlimited opportunities to learn and develop a growth mindset. Of course, you can't beat an old-fashioned book.

## Mental Energy Tips

1. Learn something new by reading one new book each month or listening to an interesting podcast.
2. Turn away from your computer or phone and give 100 percent focus when speaking with someone.
3. Eliminate distractions by intentionally focusing on one thing at a time.[18]
4. Create your own mantra to help you stay focused. I like to recite, "Make it happen!"

---

[18] Jane Harkness, "How to Monotask Your Way to a Productive Day," Freedom, January 2, 2019, https://freedom.to/blog/how-to-monotask-your-way-to-a-productive-day/.

5. Identify tools to quiet your mind—journaling, meditating, mindful walking, etc.

## Sixteen-Second Reset

I learned this technique from Jim Loehr, a professional tennis coach who went on to found a company called the Human Performance Institute in Orlando, Florida. Jim realized when working with tennis players at the highest levels that what made the difference whether they won or lost wasn't how fast their serve was or how much they practiced. It was whether they had the ability to reset their mindset between points. You might be watching a tennis player, and they will look at their racket and bounce the ball a couple of times. What they are doing is taking additional time to reset their mindset.

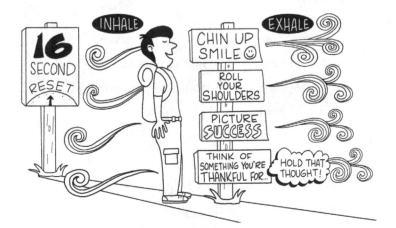

I adopted this strategy in my 1:1 coaching and group facilitation. I'll walk you through it:

1. Take a deep breath in...hold your chin up...smile big ...exhale.
2. Take a deep breath in...roll your shoulders...shake out your arms...exhale.
3. Take a deep breath in...picture success...hold that thought...exhale.
4. Take a deep breath in...think of something you are thankful for...hold that thought...exhale.

This is a quick and effective way to reset your frame of mind. You can use it in your business life—in the middle of a meeting, or when you have been staring at your computer screen for too long. Every 90 to 120 minutes, it is important to reset mentally, emotionally, and physically. Being able to reset my mind before going back to my day allows me to feel refreshed and more focused.

## SPIRITUAL ENERGY

Most executives are reluctant to address the spiritual level of the performance pyramid in a business setting, and understandably so. The word "spiritual" is often polarizing and doesn't seem immediately relevant to high performance. For some, spirituality relates directly to their religious beliefs. For others, spirituality is grounded in teachings from ancient philosophers. And still for others, it has a universal appeal and connection. Regardless, spirituality is one of the key foundations for life, and it's up to you to define yours.

For me, spiritual energy simply means the energy that is unleashed by tapping into one's deepest values and defining a strong sense of purpose. As such, it serves as a sustenance in the face of adversity and as a powerful source of motivation, focus, determination, and resilience.

One of the key sources of spiritual energy is alignment, and the result is an intentional life. When you have spiritual energy, you feel you are "in the zone," connected to something bigger than you. This helps you tap into your best self. Conversely, when you are not aligned, you will be tired, lethargic, and irritable.

Discovering your spirituality and spiritual energy is a very personal journey—unique to each individual. As such, I won't devote this section to learnings and teachings; rather, I will share a few books and sources I've found helpful, and I will share a "best self vision" practice you can use to move towards being your best self.

## Book Suggestions

*The Four Agreements: A Practical Guide to Personal Freedom*, Don Miguel Ruiz

A simple yet powerful practice to help you have peace of mind and achieve freedom from self-limiting beliefs that cause unnecessary drama and suffering.

*The Power of Now: A Guide to Spiritual Enlightenment*, Eckhart Tolle

A transformational way to become "present" and avoid the mental and emotional drama of living in the past and future—two things that only exist in our mind. Learn to thrive in the present, and live in the now.

*The Seven Spiritual Laws of Success*, Deepak Chopra

In this book, Chopra distills the essence of his teachings into seven simple, practical, yet powerful principles to help gain success in all areas of your life.

## Best Self Vision

Becoming your "best self" means double-clicking into your own head and asking some deeper questions. You can use the following questions to help you identify who you are when you are at your best, and the behaviors you exhibit during those times.

→ What truly matters most to you?

→ What fuels or energizes you? What depletes you?

→ Who are you when you are most proud of yourself?

→ How do you lead others, treat others on a daily basis, connect to family, show kindness or compassion, and display character?

→ Who are you emotionally, mentally, and physically when you are most proud of yourself?

I wrote out my best self vision: *When I am most proud of myself and when I'm at my best...*

*I am confident, I'm leading, I'm engaging, I'm inspiring other people. I have empathy and compassion.*

## The Truth about Your Best Self Vision

What percentage of time, at work and at home, do you embody your best self?

_____% at work

_____% at home

For me, it was 70 percent at work, and 70 percent at home.

When, where, how, and why do you most often fall short of your best self?

If you're not your best self 100 percent of the time (and who is?), ask yourself where you falter. For me, it's when I'm not doing things in my wheelhouse, not managing my nutrition, not drinking enough water, and not working out. That is when I fall short.

Use this exercise to focus on the opportunity to continue to grow and create the life you want.

## DAILY PRACTICES FOR MANAGING ENERGY

The following are practices I've used to increase and manage all four types of energy. Give them a try and see what they do for you.

First, I try to have a consistent morning routine. The days I feel the best and have the most energy are the days when I get a good night's sleep, don't have much (or any!) alcohol the night before, and follow my morning routine.

My routine is straightforward:

✓ 650 mL (three cups) of water right after waking up[19]
✓ Meditation or breathing exercises
✓ Gratitude
✓ Hiking, which usually lasts an hour and a half

Bonus points if I can see the sunrise, which sparks my biggest energy. There is something about a new day beginning and seeing the sunrise that helps me focus on what matters. When I was little, my mom would always tell me, "Today is the first day of the rest of your life." I used to roll my eyes in response and think it was a cheesy saying, but as an adult, I now realize that actually, she was right. Today *is* the first day of the rest of your life. Today is full of possibility, and it is up to each of us to fulfill that possibility.

---

[19] You should drink at least 650 mL (three cups) of water right after waking up. Build up your tolerance to drinking this much water day by day! Drinking water first thing in the morning helps you clean out your colon to help you absorb as many nutrients as you can from the food you eat for the rest of the day.

Throughout my day, I'll take periodic breaks. In your own schedule, find break times that work for you, but always be willing to adapt as needed. Recently, I had some Zoom meetings in Europe and Asia, which required me to start the calls at four or five in the morning. It threw my rhythm out of whack, but then I adjusted my routine. I worked in the morning and went for a hike later in the day, and eventually I figured out what could work for me, despite the changes. You, too, will experience changes in your daily routine, and it's important to listen to your body as you do. Work when you have mental energy, and then find time to get outside and relax to recharge.

Finally, I see the great outdoors as foundational to all of my energy. As Albert Einstein said, "Look deep into nature, and then you will understand everything better."

### Energy Management Assessment

This quick assessment will identify where your energy is low, highlighting what might need to be addressed in your life.

What would you do if you had more energy? _____

_____

List three words to describe your best self:

1. _____

2. _____

3. _____

Choose the response that best describes you (average over the past six months):

How much physical energy do you have?

    1 = between empty and ¼ empty

    2 = between ¼ empty and ½ full

    3 = between ½ full and ¾ full

    4 = between ¾ full and full

1. What is the quality of your emotional energy?

    1 = fully negative (toxic)

    2 = more negative than positive

    3 = more positive than negative

    4 = fully positive

2. How focused are you?

    1 = fully scattered

    2 = more scattered than focused

    3 = more focused than scattered

    4 = fully focused (laser)

3. How committed are you to your purpose?

    1 = fully uncommitted

    2 = more uncommitted than committed

    3 = more committed than uncommitted

    4 = fully committed

See where you stand:

      14–16 = fully engaged

      10–13 = partially engaged

      6–9 = partially disengaged

      Below 6 = fully disengaged

Full engagement is the ability to intentionally invest your full and best energy right here, right now.

# CHAPTER SEVEN

# Expand Your Circle of Comfort

> *"Courage is the strength to do things in spite of fear, not without fear. The only failure is not trying."*
>
> —SARA BLAKELY, FOUNDER OF SPANX

WHEN I FIRST HEARD ABOUT BRITISH ADVENTURER MILES HILTON-Barber, he was about to take the stage as a guest speaker. He had traveled all over the world, setting numerous world records across all seven continents in mountaineering; desert and polar ultra-marathons; power-boat racing; scuba-diving; motor-racing; and long distance, aerobatic, and supersonic flying. He had climbed Everest and flown the longest flight. His endless list of accomplishments was impressive. As he was about to take the stage, the emcee shared one final piece of information: Hilton-Barber had been legally blind for twenty years.

I was stunned. The life he had lived would be an accomplishment for anybody, and he was doing it without the benefit of good eyesight. His story inspired me to think of ways I can expand my own circle of comfort on a regular basis. What can I do that is unique and different, and a little uncomfortable every day, week, month, and year?

## RISK VS. COMFORT

When I hike with clients, I sometimes draw a circle in the dirt with a dot in the center that represents them. I explain that they are the dot—the dominant middle—and the circle is their comfort zone. Every time they step outside that circle, they will feel uncomfortable, scared, or nervous. Then I draw a second, larger circle. I explain that every time they step outside the circle, it gets bigger. Their comfort capacity increases.

We all have a natural inclination to retreat back to our comfort zone as fast as we can, but if we can sit in discomfort, we can grow and learn. There is no growth in comfort, and no comfort in growth.

Risk is a concept we hear a lot about, especially in business and especially as it relates to reward. What if you're not actually experiencing risk, but discomfort? Rock climbing is considered a risky activity, but climbers are harnessed in and attached by a rope to a professional belay to counterbalance them if they fall. So, climbing isn't actually that dangerous, in terms of injury or death, but the discomfort level can be high for a first-timer. If you frame stepping outside your circle of comfort as a risk, you are less likely to take that action than if you realize you are simply challenging your level of comfort.

When my kids were little, I explained to them that as parents, our job is to help them get their circle of comfort as big as possible. That meant taking risks, being uncomfortable, and not being afraid to fail.

Most kids are asked questions like, "What was the best part of your day?" or "What did you learn at school today?" Sara Blakely, founder of the billion-dollar hosiery and apparel company Spanx, had a bit of a different dinnertime experience growing up.

"My dad used to ask my brother and me at the dinner table what we had failed at that week," she told the audience at a Network for Teaching Entrepreneurship event in New York City.[20] She went on: "I can remember coming home from school and saying, 'Dad, I tried out for this and I was horrible!' and he would high-five me and say, 'Way to go!' If I didn't have something that I had failed at, he actually would be disappointed."

This dinner table tradition allowed Blakely to see the value in failure. "My dad always encouraged me to fail, and because of this, he gave me the gift of retraining my thinking about failure," she explained. "Failure for me became about not trying, instead of the outcome."

Having never taken a business class and having zero background in the fashion retail industry, Blakely's investment in Spanx forced her out of her circle of comfort, to say the least. Her decision to go for it ultimately paid off. In addition to being named by *Forbes* as the world's youngest self-made female billionaire in 2012 when she was forty-one, Blakely also made *Time* magazine's prestigious 100 Most Influential People list that year.

How can you reframe possibilities before you? How can you see the next step as a way to move outside your circle of comfort rather than as risk-taking? Yes, risk might be involved, but at a deeper level you are being called to expand, to grow.

---

[20] Kathleen Elkins, "The Surprising Dinner Table Question that Got Billionaire Sara Blakey to Where She Is Today," *Business Insider,* April 3, 2015. https://www.businessinsider.com/the -blakely-family-dinner-table-question-2015-3.

## Emotions Cause Action

One of the best ways I know of to step outside your circle of comfort is by taking action spontaneously and without warning. This forces you or your team to respond to emotions. You have no time for overthinking, which can leave you in paralysis.

I saw the value of taking this kind of action when I was brought in as a consultant for Alcon, a medical company specializing in eye care products. Thirty people were working in the omni-channel marketing department divided between two divisions: corporate communications and brand communications. Each division oversaw twenty or thirty different brands, with each brand having their own website and social media channels. Each had different key performance indicators; one wanted to drive traffic, the other wanted to drive engagement. There was no overall leader and no common strategy. Each division was essentially competing with the others.

One of the key objectives set before me was to develop an aligned strategy and build trust between corporate and brand communications so they were one team moving in the same direction.

After a bit of time getting a lay of the land, I had an idea. I wanted to create something provocative that would get the team to think differently, and unite them around a particular issue. Nothing unites people like a crisis, so I decided to stage a viral hoax. My daughter helped me mock up a fake Twitter and an Instagram handle for Kim Kardashian, who had 70 million followers at the time.

We took to the Internet and found two images: one of Ms. Kardashian rubbing her eye, and another less flattering image where it looked like she was recovering from surgery or just waking up. I began my virtual meeting with thirty people in the Alcon social media department. After the introduction and a few icebreaker activities, I executed my plan. I started by saying, "I don't know if you realize, but there was some good news last week. Kim Kardashian was fitted with the new Dailies Total 1 contact lenses at a LensCrafters in Santa Monica, California." I was completely fabricating this story. You could see the expression on people's faces. This room of digital media people knew what an impact having an endorsement from Kim Kardashian could mean to the brand. A ripple went through the room. They were excited.

"However," I continued, "there's a problem. And one of the reasons we are meeting today is to talk about this."

I pulled up the first image, and I read it out loud.

> My eye doctor said I would love Dailies TOTAL1 contact lenses. WRONG!! I can't get them out of my eyes. Worst ever, never buy @Alcon #neveragain.

I let that sink in. People weren't sure how to react. I could see the concern on everyone's faces...panic was setting in.

I continued. "It gets worse. This morning I saw this post." Then I showed them the "post-surgery" post.

Alcon Dailies TOTAL1 Contacts are the worst I have ever tried. They irritate my eyes, and I can't get them out! Waste of money! Do not buy if you don't want contacts stuck in your eye...

Without giving the team time to react, I set up three breakout rooms and moved them immediately into solution-mode. "I want you to figure this out together: What do we do? How do we communicate? What's our next step? We'll meet back here in twenty minutes."

It worked so well that I got a call on my cell phone from the head of digital a few minutes later. "Bart, I love it," he said. "That stunt worked a little too well. There are already people crafting text messages to the CEO to alert him. They think it's real."

Eventually, I had to tell the team that none of this was true, but the ruse still worked. It got people outside of their comfort zone and forced them to think on their feet. Could this stunt have backfired? Sure. I pushed the envelope, but it cut to the heart of that entire team's emotions. People were horrified, aggrieved, and embarrassed. And those emotions galvanized a team. They weren't "in corporate communications" anymore; they weren't "in charge of the Instagram feed" for that contact lens; they were one team, focused on a common problem. They were all Alcon, united to do damage control to limit the effects of some bad public relations. *Seventy million people just saw a major influencer with a contact lens stuck in her eye, and they think it's our fault. What do we do?* They were one team for the first time.

Once the exercise was over, we all laughed. No boring death by PowerPoint presentations here.

This approach can apply to any business, and any industry. I have found that a bold move from your competitor or a crisis can catapult a team into action. It will create team unity and get people thinking differently, outside their normal constraints. It provides opportunities for them to grow and prosper.

## Taking the Leap

I'll never forget when I first had an idea for screening kiosks. I knew this idea would challenge me to take a leap in a whole new direction.

It was 2004, and I was working in the eye care division of Novartis, living in England on an international assignment. I was the National Account Manager, selling contact lenses to national retailers. Walmart (called ASDA in the United Kingdom) was my largest customer. As the category leader in contact lenses, they wanted us to find a way to drive traffic from the stores into the Vision Center. While the ASDA stores were highly successful, shoppers were not utilizing the in-store Vision Centers. Maybe they didn't even know they were there.

In February 2004, we scheduled an off-site meeting to brainstorm ideas. We had consultants come in to help us determine how to drive traffic to the ASDA Vision Centers. I was in the back of the room, listening, when the idea hit me, "What if we had a kiosk that could screen your vision?" I asked. "It would tell you if you have 20/20 vision and, if not, it would print out a report and tell you to go get an eye exam."

There were lots of nodding heads in the room. "Oh yeah, that's a cool idea," someone said.

And I said, "No, no, no, that's *the* idea!" *The* idea. I couldn't get it out of my head. I wrote the basis of the business plan that very evening. I spent nights and weekends brainstorming and devising a plan, then started communicating back and forth with the executive ranks in the US about the idea. Finally, the general counsel said we should file a patent for the kiosk.

I finished my two-year assignment in England and returned to the US excited to continue my work with Novartis. My official job with the company gave me the autonomy and flexibility to work on this passion project of self-service eye care kiosks, while continuing to establish and build relationships with the executive team. For two more years, I incubated the business that would become SoloHealth. I had always been entrepreneurial. I knew this business did not belong inside Novartis. I wanted to change the way eye care was delivered, and I knew it wasn't going to survive internally, but I kept pressing on. Big companies have a lot of resources, and I was tapping into as many as I could—sales, marketing, logistics, market research.

One day, the head of business development and the general counsel set up a meeting; it was an intervention. They sat me down and said, "Bart, we like you, we love the project, and we love your passion, but we don't invest in things that plug in the wall. Novartis is a drug company. If this is really something you want to pursue, we would consider spinning it out."

I was happy to hear this, because that had been my plan all along.

They told me they had to get the CEO's approval, which would likely take a month to get. For the next month, I continued to build these relationships. When I finally met with the CEO, the head of business development, and the general counsel, I pitched my idea. Instead of firing me, the CEO said, "This is exactly the type of thing we should be working on." Instead of spinning it out, he gave me a $1 million budget and a full-time job to work on developing this self-service kiosk. I would report to the head of business development from then on.

I was excited until I realized just how slowly big companies move. The general counsel pulled me aside after the meeting and let me know that even though the CEO had allocated a $1 million budget, anything over half a million dollars had to be approved through their internal budget review process, which wasn't until September. This was June. *What was I going to do for the next three months?*

I couldn't wait three months just to get budget approval! Time was of the essence. Most people would have resigned themselves to wait and "hope" to get approval. But not me. I had an idea. For that budget approval meeting, I wanted to have a prototype already built. The general counsel said, "Bart, you don't have a budget yet, and you have another full-time job right now. How on earth are you going to get a prototype built?" The general counsel happened to run the business development department and oversaw the budget for that department. I asked him if he had a slush fund. He said, "Look, I could probably squirrel away $50,000 for you. Would that help?" Now, 50 grand wasn't going to go very far, but I said, "Absolutely, $50,000 will help. Thank you."

But I knew I couldn't stop there if I wanted to make this idea a reality. So, I went to the President of North America and had the same conversation. Then I repeated that process three more times. I had lunch with a total of five different executives and asked each one of them if they had $50,000. I had already invested time building the relationships, so this was my equivalent of Harvey Mackay's 2:00 a.m. phone call. Each of them committed $50,000 to my prototype budget, all within three days.

I went back to the head of Business Development and asked his assistant to set up a separate budget center. After all, I was a sales guy working out of my home office. She agreed, and that same hour, I emailed the five executives and their assistants. "Pursuant to the lunch discussion, please transfer the $50,000 into this budget center." I now had $250,000 and a budget center nobody knew about—*inside Novartis*. (I had to wait ten years to tell this story.)

I hired an external hardware company, a software company, a product design firm, a finance person, and—since I wasn't supposed to be working on this—a project manager, and work began in earnest on having the prototype built.

When the prototype came in, I approached the head of facilities on the loading dock and told him my plan: I wanted to stage the prototype outside the boardroom and asked if he could help me. He replied, "Yeah, our guys will be in at 10:00 a.m." And I said, "Well, actually, I'd love it to be staged before anyone gets to work." There was a pause. I could tell by the way he looked at me that he thought I was a little crazy. I told him I would buy his guys pizza for lunch. How about that? He smiled and said, "Sure."

It cost me a whopping fifteen dollar pizza to get my kiosk situated outside the boardroom. To create an element of mystery and surprise, I covered the kiosk with a car cover I had bought the night before. The final detail was to make a sign that read, "CONFIDENTIAL DO NOT TOUCH." It was very theatrical, but I wanted it to be memorable.

And it worked.

People filed into the board meeting to make a decision on whether or not to approve the $1 million budget to start building the proto-type. My thirty-minute slot turned into an hour because they realized they needed more time to discuss whether to get into this business. I was patient, keeping quiet about the prototype. Obviously they had seen the covered object sitting outside the boardroom, but they didn't know what it was. I waited until the end of the meeting and after the budget had been approved, I said, "Guys, I'd love you to see the first prototype." Everyone filed outside, and I whipped the car cover off like a magician.

The CEO sat down at the kiosk and was the first to try it out.

It was one of the proudest moments of my career. Through pure tenacity, I had been able to get the first vision screening kiosk built. Sure, I was totally pushing the envelope. Could I have gotten fired? Maybe. But I had done it! I had gotten results. I had "dug my well," taken risks, and stepped outside my comfort zone. And it all paid off.

For me, it was a win-win: If the budget had not been approved that day, I would have walked away with a prototype I could use to spin into my own company. I saw the value in this idea, even if nobody else did, and I stood behind it.

## Your Plan to Fail

If you step out of your circle of comfort, what is the worst thing that can happen? For me, the worst thing that could happen was that I might fail. After two years of developing these eye care kiosks within Novartis, I was ready to leave and start my own company: SoloHealth. Once again, I was taking the leap! It felt scary. Someone challenged me to imagine that I completely failed at the endeavor I was about to take on. I expanded on the idea and created the Plan to Fail.

It works like this: Write down everything that would happen if you were to fail, on one page. This is your worst-case scenario. For example, you might have to lay off employees, call your investors, call your bank, or share your failure with your spouse and family. Reflect on your own worst-case scenario. My guess is that it will help you gain the perspective you need. You might realize that what you're about to take on is not going to be fun, but you won't die. Everything will be okay. In a worst-case scenario, you can rebuild. Catastrophizing a situation without truly thinking through a worst-case scenario prevents us from taking action. It keeps us in our circle of comfort.

The night before I was going to hand in my resignation to start the company that would become SoloHealth, I felt fear and discomfort about leaving a big company with the resources, the company car, the benefits, the salary, and all the friends I had made. Giving that up for a tiny office, to start my own company, was definitely stepping out of my circle of comfort. But I knew that to have the personal freedom I wanted, I'd need to build something myself.

This was a powerful moment in my life. I distinctly remember getting a bottle of champagne and taking Aly to the empty parking lot of the Novartis headquarters, a building that houses three thousand people. I looked up at the flagpole, and we toasted. I said, "This is it."

I had written my own Plan to Fail the week before I resigned. The truth was I didn't know if I'd be successful, but I knew that I would be okay. I knew I would be in control of my life. It was a step toward an intentional life, and I was not going to succumb to pressures of comfort. I would move ahead, knowing I could fail, but knowing at the same time that this step could change my life forever. And sure enough, it did.

### Exercise: Worst-case Scenario

When you're faced with a difficult decision, or you're feeling apprehensive about starting something new, ask yourself, What if I fail? What is the worst-case scenario? Write down all the things that would happen when you fail.

Reflect on what you have written. For example, are you willing to do what it takes and risk possible failure to pursue your dream? Are you able to let the possibility fuel you rather than freeze you? Now is the time to be completely honest with yourself. You need to fully acknowledge the realities before you, so that you go into the new steps with fire in your belly.

## Grow Your Circle

In Chapter One, I told you about the zip code strategy, which Aly and I used to start living a more intentional life in Boulder. This was due in large part to wanting to move beyond our circle of comfort. In a very literal way, we were being challenged to grow our circle.

We had spent our lives checking boxes to fulfill the model of success we had grown up with: we were living in the suburbs of Atlanta, had two kids, good health, played golf twice a week, and made a great salary. We felt like we had it all. Life was great. It was really, really comfortable.

The problem was that we felt *too* comfortable. Were we truly growing and being challenged? Was getting together with the same friends, drinking beer and talking about football, week in and week out, all there was for my wife and me? We didn't have the deeper connections we craved, and we knew we had to step outside the circle.

To start moving outside your circle, here's a first step you can take: write down three ways you wish you could grow, things you've always said you wanted to do. The list should give you butterflies. If it doesn't, you're still inside your comfort zone. After you write the list, make a plan of action, and share the list and the plan with someone you trust for accountability. Make progress each day, even if it's small, but keep moving forward. You'll be amazed at what you can do and overcome if you simply take the next step.

Nature, in all her wisdom, has a lot to teach us about moving outside our circle of comfort. Take, for example, the mother eagle that pushes her babies out of the nest to learn to fly. It seems cruel, but in reality that push, as scary and risky as it seems, is exactly what baby eagles need to learn to soar. And as scary as pushing yourself out of your comfort zone may seem, it's exactly what you need to soar, too.

# CHAPTER EIGHT

# Identifying Your Ideal Environment

> *"The future isn't a place that we're going to go, it's a place that you get to create."*
>
> —NANCY DUARTE

I REMEMBER SITTING WITH ALY ON THE ROOFTOP OF THE RIO Grande Mexican restaurant, overlooking the foothills on the west side of Boulder. Having just left the 90 degrees and stifling humidity in Atlanta, we were enjoying the crisp, 65-degree July evening. We each sipped a margarita and looked at each other without saying a word as the sun set over the Flatirons, turning the sky purple and pink. We nodded and smiled. We both knew it: this was the setting for our next chapter.

Within a month, the kids were enrolled in school, and we had sold our house, our cars, and half of all our other material possessions. We didn't know a single person in Boulder, but our minds were made up.

## ZIP CODE STRATEGY

The "zip code strategy" my mentor had suggested to us was simple: pick where you want to live first and figure out the details from there.

We thought once we had decided to move to Boulder, the rest would fall into place, but it wasn't quite that simple. We needed to take intentional action and use creative problem-solving. Boulder had a very low inventory of housing available. Houses were being snapped up before they even hit the market. After that night of deciding this was the place for us, we realized we'd only be in town for thirty-six more hours. The next day, we set out to look for places to rent and couldn't find anything. When the day was coming to an end and we didn't have any good options, I started to wonder if we should rethink our plan. *Why are we doing this?* I wondered.

Aly wasn't deterred. She picked up a bottle of wine, got the kids settled with a movie in our room, and the two of us went to the lobby to devise our next steps. I came up with the idea to search for all of the houses for sale that met our criteria and that had been on the market for more than ninety days. If they couldn't sell their home, maybe they would be willing to rent it to us.

I created a flyer telling our story, what we were looking for, with a photo of our family. I emphasized that we would take the best care of the owner's house like it was our own.

The next morning, we drove to all of the houses on our list. Most people weren't home, so I left the flyer on their doorstep. When I did get to meet the owner or the neighbors, I had the kids roll down the window and wave. "That's my family," I said. "We are looking for a house to rent." Still, we didn't get any bites.

When the last day of our trip was coming to an end, I was starting to lose hope that we could pull off a quick move. Then I got a call. "We'll rent our house to you," the voice on the other end of the line said. "We thought it would sell by now but since it hasn't, we are willing to rent it to you for six months." We hurried back to the house and shook hands with the owner before heading to the airport.

\* \* \*

The zip code strategy compelled us to look into identifying attributes that mattered to us as a family. It just so happened that our answers required us to move, but the concept does not limit itself to geographical changes. It's more about being intentional and creating a life you love. At its core, the zip code strategy is about gaining a clear understanding of what you want, your values, and what fires you up mentally, emotionally, physically—and then intentionally going after it.

Even if you aren't planning to move right now, you can tap into the power of the zip code strategy by taking a step back and reflecting on what is truly most valuable to you. What do you *really* care about? When you are your happiest and best self, what are you doing?

My wife and I took our first steps by creating the list of attributes that mattered the most to us, which I shared in Chapter One. You can apply this exercise to any domain of life. What is ideal for you when it comes to work, your relationships, or how you learn? Are these domains aligned with your values? If not, it's time to become more intentional.

## LIVING MORE INTENTIONALLY

Even more important than changing our physical space is changing our mindset.

To learn about how to get set up for success in this area, I interviewed my friend Erin Pheil. Erin is the founder of The MindFix Group, a boutique consulting and coaching company that helps entrepreneurs and leaders get unstuck and thrive through extraordinarily effective, one-on-one rapid transformation programs.

The programs at MindFix quickly and effectively erase issues that people often spend years trying to work out in therapy, such as patterns of self-sabotage, mental blocks, and negative emotions. In other words, MindFix helps people get out of their own way and achieve what they desire–with significantly less time and effort than traditional methods of self-improvement.

If we want to improve our lives, to be more purposeful and more conscious, it's critical to develop an awareness of our limiting beliefs and patterns—those thoughts and behaviors that we repeat over and over unconsciously that aren't serving us.

"We often experience patterns of thought, emotion, or behaviors that are counterproductive to the way we want to live," Erin explained. "We may want to feel happiness, joy, or love, but our mind is holding onto old beliefs that directly block us from experiencing these things, or it keeps us locked into negative patterns. That's why, to live more purposefully, it's imperative that we become aware of these beliefs."

Erin went on to share that whether we experience patterns of anxiety, avoidance, procrastination, or hypercriticism, we all have the capacity to shift from seeing ourselves as someone to whom things happen, to someone with agency and choice.

"Seeing ourselves as humans experiencing counterproductive patterns (versus humans who are 'just a certain way') is empowering, as it means we have an ability to change what doesn't serve us," she continued.

"Instead of feeling broken or resigned or as if there's nothing that can be done about our patterns, we can see them as roadblocks in our way, and we all have the capability of removing these roadblocks."

## Uncovering the Million Dollar Question

Erin told me about a simple exercise her team uses with their clients to help people uncover why they experience counterproductive patterns. She invites them to ask themselves this:

What would I have to believe to be true in order to keep experiencing this pattern over and over again?

This "million dollar" question helps us quickly get down to the root of our repeated thoughts, emotions, or behaviors. It allows us to see how much of our life experience is not based upon an "objective" reality but rather what we believe to be true.

"Our beliefs directly impact—and are often the root cause of—what we think, how we feel, and how we act in the world," Erin explained.

"When we ask ourselves this million dollar question, we often uncover a gold mine within our own minds! This is because the question can help us identify the hidden root causes preventing us from being able to step into our full potential. Beliefs people hold that prevent them from living up to their capacity might be, 'If I make a mistake or fail, I will be rejected,' or, 'I'm not good enough. I'm not capable. I'm not important.'"

Even if we consciously disagree with these beliefs, our subconscious may still hold onto them. For example, consider how you might feel if someone came up to you and said, "You're not good enough." Sure, you might argue or refute that statement and say, "Yes, I am." But there could still be a little part of you deep down that believes what the person said might be true. This small irritation then causes a ripple effect outward, and creates friction and problems in our lives.

Erin went on to suggest that these beliefs act as lines of programming, continually running in the background of your mind. *Don't do it! You're not good enough! Don't do it! You're not good enough!* And we spend a large portion of our energy trying to fight against this programming all day long. We often have to pump ourselves up and push through fear and resistance. This uses up valuable life force and energy.

So, what's the solution? What can we do?

We have more answers available to us than we might think. Erin explained that in the last few decades, a variety of new methods have been developed that allow us to delete problematic mind programming and beliefs in methodical, consistent ways.

"This mental programming and these limiting beliefs, which we often picked up when we were young, CAN be shifted," she told me. "For some people, beliefs like, 'That's just how I am,' 'That's how I think,' 'That's how I was raised, or 'It's in my DNA' can be shifted by simply uncovering them. For others, a bit of assistance might be needed—having someone help you in clearing out these beliefs and programs is necessary so they no longer bother you."

I asked Erin to walk us through an example of how someone might begin to shift their beliefs so they can live more intentionally. She described how she might work with someone whose pattern is to overwork and never slow down. I have outlined her explanation in the following section. If you put yourself in the shoes of the workaholic, you'll be able to see how this deprogramming process could work for you in any area of your life.

## From False Beliefs to Freedom

If you're stuck in a pattern that is not serving you, it's likely there are beliefs acting like mental programs running in the background of your mind, causing you to continue this pattern—whether you're aware of these beliefs or not.

Let's say you regularly work twelve-hour days, and can't seem to stop doing so, even though you know your actions are increasing stress, relationship problems, and health issues in your life.

Let's walk through a simple step-by-step process to explore how your compulsive working pattern could be related to what you believe.

**Step One:** Get a clear picture and understanding of the pattern that doesn't serve you. What is actually happening? What do you actually do (or think or feel) that is causing you frustration? Use very specific language, details, and numbers. You want to pinpoint and define an exact pattern—because you won't be able to shift it if it's too broad.

For example, "I'm a workaholic" is a label, not a clear, specific pattern. The statement is too generic and is therefore not useful when it comes to being able to change what's not working in your life.

"If my business' checking account balance drops below $500,000, I feel anxious, start having thoughts that I'm not capable enough, and can't allow myself to leave work before 8:00 p.m." is far more specific and useful. It is a specific pattern that we can work with.

When you see your challenge as a pattern (instead of something that you "just are"), you understand it is not you—but instead a repeated experience that can be changed.

Take a few minutes now to get curious about your behavior and clearly identify a pattern that isn't serving you.

**Step Two:** Ask yourself: Do I actually want to change this pattern? It's important to do this before you explore what might be underneath your pattern.

Erin explained that there have been occasions in the past where her team worked with someone for weeks and they still experienced resistance to change. Oftentimes, they'll get to a point where they say, "You know what? Now that I think about it, I don't really want to change this about myself. I don't actually want to let this pattern go."

This step is obviously critical to the process, and the response needs to be genuine. If you don't want to change, you won't, and in that case you simply need to acknowledge that pattern will be there until you truly want something different.

So, you can save yourself time by first asking yourself if you are truly interested in letting go of your pattern. If you get a "Yes" answer, proceed to Step Three.

**Step Three:** Let's generate a list of the possible mental programming (beliefs) that could be behind your pattern. Ask yourself the million dollar question: what would I have to believe to be true in order to keep (doing X)? In our example here about not being able to stop working twelve-hour days, this question would be, "What would I have to believe to be true in order to keep working twelve-hour days, even when it's hurting me?"

Brainstorm a list on paper.

To help you with this process, here is a list of possible beliefs that might keep you stuck repeating the pattern of behavior noted in Step Two:

- What makes me valuable is working hard.
- What makes me important is working hard.
- What makes me worthy is working hard.
- To be successful, you must work long hours.
- If you're not working long hours, you're lazy.
- In order to make a good living/a lot of money, I must work hard.
- What makes me worthy is working a lot.
- Success requires struggle.

- I'm not capable.
- I'm not good enough.
- I'm a fake, fraud, or phony.
- It's got to be hard.
- Success isn't deserved unless hard work is involved.
- Success can't come easy.
- I can't trust others to do a good job.
- No one can do things as well as I can.
- If I don't do things myself, they won't get done.
- In order to be a good leader, I must work harder/longer than my team.
- If I'm relaxing or not working, I'm lazy.
- If I'm relaxing or not working, I'm bad.
- The harder I work, the more money I make.

Keep in mind you may consciously disagree with some of the beliefs causing your patterns. It's possible that only a part of you may be holding on to them and, if this is the case, it's important to be able to acknowledge that part of you. This self-honesty is absolutely critical; you can't shift your mindset until you can first admit to yourself what you, or part of you, believes to be true.

**Step Four:** Review the list in front of you. Say each belief out loud to yourself. If any part of you believes the statement to be true, you will likely have some type of reaction—even if small. You might feel slightly sad or anxious. You might notice a subtle physical sensation in your body. Some people say their stomach tenses up or their throat tightens.

Contrast these subtle reactions to what happens when you verbalize a silly statement that no part of you believes, such as "I am a giraffe." Notice you have no reaction, other than a possible chuckle, when you make such a statement.

**Step Five:** Engage in a short thought experiment:

1. Choose one of the beliefs from your list that feels strongest to you.
2. Close your eyes and take a deep breath.
3. Imagine that belief being completely gone from your mind when you wake up tomorrow morning.

Try it out now. Take thirty seconds to quiet yourself and relax, and then imagine what it would be like waking up tomorrow without that belief. (Focus on the beliefs and patterns that are relevant to you if the example of the workaholic is not.) Try it with as many beliefs from your list as you like. For many, this is a fast, powerful experiment.

While this exercise won't necessarily clear away your problematic programming or belief for good, it WILL give you a glimpse into what it feels like as if they were gone, which is eye-opening for most.

Many people experience a profound sense of relief when they experience what it would be like if the beliefs were no longer looping in their minds. This final step shows you how you would suddenly feel and act differently. It shows you what is possible.

You can use this process any time you want to start down the road of changing your beliefs and transforming your life. You don't have to be stuck. You don't have to keep looping in circles that don't serve you.

Following this exercise, the process of actually clearing these beliefs from your mind (instead of just imagining they're gone) can feel a bit like trying to scratch your own back. Your brain has constructed roadblocks to make it challenging for you to change what you believe to be true. The great news is that it's absolutely possible with some help. Erin's team specializes in helping people do exactly this.

When I tried this exercise for myself, I realized I had a fear of being judged. I was worried about what other people thought of me and my actions. In fact, this pattern prevented me from writing this book for more than three years. After working with Erin, however, I had an epiphany—I realized that I did not need to worry about what others thought of me. I could eliminate these negative thoughts and press forward with confidence and conviction.

> *"I have looked in the mirror every morning and asked myself:*
> *If today were the last day of my life, would I want to do what*
> *I am about to do today? And whenever the answer has been*
> *'No' for too many days in a row, I know I need to change*
> *something."*
>
> —STEVE JOBS

# JOB CRAFTING

Sometimes finding your ideal environment means shifting your focus within your work environment. Many people think they should get a new job when they are unhappy with their current employment. That may feel like your only option, but it shouldn't be a knee-jerk reaction. My experience is that this is often a simple case of "grass is greener syndrome," the idea that there is always something better that we are missing.

Rather than experiencing stability, security, and satisfaction in the present environment, the feeling is there is more and better elsewhere, and anything less than ideal won't do. Chances are, the problems you are experiencing in your current employment will follow you to your next one. Instead, look at ways to stay where you are and water the grass you are on. Transform your environment!

Again, this comes back to being intentional, and ensuring the elements in your life are happening *by* you instead of *to* you. I would encourage you to reframe your relationship with your work: Instead of leaving to find a new job, create an opportunity in the job you already have. Look at the trends, look at things that people *aren't* doing. Look at your unique ability, your Zone of Genius, and your personal values. Then see if you can create something new where you are.

In his book, *Think Again: The Power of Knowing What You Don't Know*, Adam Grant writes about two colleagues, James Dunton and Amy Remeski. "In every line of work, there are people who become active architects of their own jobs...they rethink their roles through job crafting. Changing their daily actions to better fit their values, interests, and skills." You can change your job or switch careers, certainly, but you can also follow the example of Dunton and Remeski, making small adjustments in your current role that breathe new meaning into your days.

Imagine you're dissatisfied in your current role, so you decide to search for a VP of sales job at a different company. You read job descriptions online, and realize that they all include all of the same responsibilities and tasks that don't appeal to you in your current position. So, you start to wonder what might happen if you could reframe your current position and craft a new role for yourself without jumping to another company. You might even approach Human Resources with your personal values, your unique abilities, and your Zone of Genius and start discussing possibilities.

For example, if you are great at sales and interacting with customers, but unskilled at creating presentations or financial spreadsheets, you might try to re-craft your position so that you can focus more on selling and less on back-office administrative tasks. This isn't about shirking responsibilities and dumping them on others; it's about playing to your strengths and working in your Zone of Genius. Remember my advisor's "digital baseball card" exercise? By finding out what's on your "baseball card," you actually make room for others on your team to switch to tasks that fit their strengths as well. In the end, this makes the whole team happier and more productive.

It's also important to remember that the future of work will be remote and hybrid. The employees of tomorrow will want to have more flexibility and autonomy, so learning to job-craft for yourself and others is simply a way to be a step ahead in the game. There will be more and more opportunities for unique job descriptions, leveraging each other's strengths.

Here's the takeaway: If you are not happy in your current role, you don't have to quit. If you can pivot within your career, your company will benefit because they will retain your experience and knowledge. Meanwhile, you will feel more satisfied and fulfilled. If you're willing to think outside of the box, it is possible to craft a position for yourself that creates a win-win for you and your employer.

## Different Vantage Point

There's a mountain near my house in Boulder called Mount Sanitas. I can hike up the hill for ten minutes and see the whole city. Every once in a while, I run into cloud inversions when I hike. That's when the normal temperature distribution of air—warm at the bottom, cooler as it moves up—gets reversed. This means that a cold layer of air is trapped at ground level, causing a lot of fog. Sometimes it's so foggy on the ground that I can't see twenty yards in front of me. Climbing the hill offers an entirely different vantage point. Half a mile up, I break through the clouds into crystal blue sky and bright sun, with the clouds below. This is always a reminder to me that we don't know what is waiting for us at the top unless we make the climb.

In business and life, a different vantage point is often necessary. Things are not always what they seem. You may be dealing with a situation that is murky. You don't know how you're going to get through it, and you can't see around the corner. Something unexpected like COVID-19 happens, and you find yourself letting employees go, and running out of cash. But if you can keep climbing up the mountain a little bit further to see the situation from a different perspective, there is a whole new view waiting for you.

One easy way to gain a new perspective is by talking to someone in your same position or role in a different industry. Seeing your situation through an objective lens can give you brand new insights.

With new vision, you are better positioned to create the life you want to live.

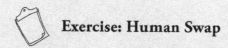 **Exercise: Human Swap**

When you encounter an opportunity, challenge, or difficult decision, think of a person in your life who you admire and respect. Imagine if they were faced with the same issue. What would they do?

A variation of this for corporations is called "Brand Takeover." Imagine your company is faced with an opportunity or a threat. Now imagine your company was taken over by another larger company (e.g., Amazon, Apple, Facebook, Nordstrom, etc.). Your company now has all the resources and people of the bigger company. What would you do differently? How would you react?

Seeing from this new vantage point can be the key to getting unstuck.

While it is important to consider the zip code strategy if you are ready for a big move, remember that you don't have to physically move to create your ideal environment. Building an intentional life is so much more than just picking where you want to live; it's about identifying how you can thrive in every area of life.

# CHAPTER NINE

# Regret Minimization

> *"Making a big life change is pretty scary.*
> *But know what's even scarier? Regret."*
>
> —ZIG ZIGLAR

WHEN I WAS GROWING UP, MY FAMILY DROVE DOWN TO FLORIDA from Illinois every Christmas. After the first week, my Dad would check in with his office and invariably come back and say, "Everything is okay at work. We're going to stay another week." And we would go *wild with glee*. Every year, we were so excited about this news.

Recently, I asked my dad if he and my mom always knew we would be staying in Florida for two weeks. He said that he liked to have "options." They always had two weeks reserved, but he didn't want to tell us in case his work schedule got too busy, or we had to go back home for any reason. This gave them the flexibility to pull the ripcord. Plus, my dad loved to surprise us.

Of course, what we were excited about was more time: more time outside, more time in paradise, more time relaxing. *More time with each other.*

Time is our biggest commodity, and yet so many business executives don't schedule time for their priorities. Recently, I was having dinner with the president of a global healthcare company. He asked me how I forecasted my business. It felt like an odd question to me because I *don't* forecast my business; that's not how I think about it. What he really wanted to know was how I decided what to work on and how I spent my time. I told him that I focus on scheduling the things I want to do with the people I love, respect, and learn from the most. I have a short list of people who bring me energy, and I want to spend time with them every month, so I schedule that time first.

His eyes lit up. "Oh, my gosh," he said. "I've been in the corporate world for thirty years. I always just wake up, my admin tells me what meetings I have scheduled for the day, and I go from meeting to meeting. I'm in service to others all day. So, you're saying that you focus on what's important to you first and then everything else follows?"

To me it was so obvious, but not for him. To him, it was a revelation.

> *"Time is what we want most, but what we use worst."*
>
> —WILLIAM PENN

Many people bounce through life without being intentional about the decisions they make. They are doing what other people want, making decisions that are not true to who they are and what makes them happy. In this chapter, we'll look at the different ways to prioritize with intentionality by using frameworks like Regret Minimization and Hell Yes or No.

## SCHEDULE LIFE FIRST

What if we measured life in events instead of in time? To do this, you can start by considering how long you have left for any given event. For example, I am currently forty-seven years old, and if I live to be eighty-five, I have thirty-seven more years, or 13,505 days.

# AN 85-YEAR HUMAN LIFE IN YEARS

# AN 85-YEAR HUMAN LIFE IN DAYS

Next, you can begin to look at all of the individual experiences you have left based on the time you have. For example, if I swim in the ocean once a year, that's thirty-seven more swims.

## IF I SWIM IN THE OCEAN ONCE A YEAR

If I hike to see the sunrise once a month, that's 444 more sunrises.

Recently, I have been thinking from this lens about my parents, who are in their late seventies. I was visiting my father last year, who I only see twice a year, and it hit me that if he hypothetically only has five years to live, I will only see him ten more times.

Most people spend a little of almost every day with their parents until they are eighteen. That was true for me, too. After leaving for college and starting my career, however, I've seen them an average of two times a year, for an average of two days each visit. If the four days a year measurement holds, that leaves me with twenty days to hang with mom and dad.

A number of years ago, Aly and I were in a seminar and the first slide read, "How many spring breaks and summers do you have left before your oldest child goes to college?" For us, it was eight years, which meant eight spring breaks and eight summers. It really hit home. Time is passing, that's inevitable; but we still have an opportunity to make the most of the time we have left with our children.

When you look at that reality, you realize that despite not being at the end of your life, you may very well be nearing the end of your time with some of your most important people. By the time my kids graduate from high school, I will have already spent 93 percent of the total time I will have with them. If you have kids, how many spring breaks and summers do you have left before your oldest child goes to college? How about weekends?

Here is a chart showing how many weekends you have with your kids from zero to eighteen years old. Fill in how many weekends you have already spent with your oldest child. How many do you have left?

# WEEKENDS LEFT WITH KIDS

Shade in the age of your oldest kid on the chart below.

☐ **= One Weekend**

All unshaded boxes represent how many weekends
you have left with your kids.
(Two Rows = 1 Year )

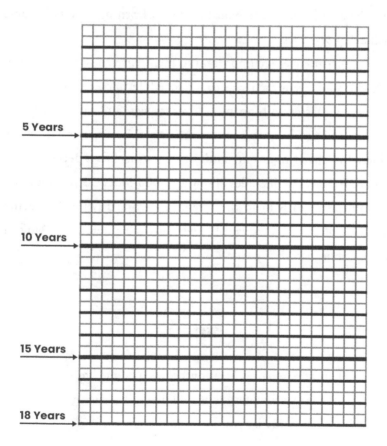

5 Years

10 Years

15 Years

18 Years

*"No one on his deathbed ever said, 'I wish I had spent more time on my business.'"*

—PAUL TSONGAS

Entrepreneur Jesse Itzler came up with the "Build Your Life Resume" concept, which I love to use in my life and with my clients. The idea is to focus your time so that you are doing the things you love with the people you love most, learning new skills, and achieving *big* goals.

Life experiences are important to me. I have chosen to add one life-changing event each year to my schedule, and one mini adventure each quarter with people I love, respect, and can learn from. Assuming I can keep this up for the next thirty years, that means thirty life changing events and 120 amazing life experiences are ahead. For me, that includes hiking a 14,000-foot peak in Colorado, running Rim-to-Rim in the Grand Canyon, driving the Pacific Coast Highway in a convertible with my daughter, and sailing in the Caribbean with my wife.

 **Exercise**

1. In the next twelve months, what is one life experience that you would like to have with someone that you love and respect?

2. What is one meaningful step you could take that would move you toward making this a reality?

For example, you might say, I would like to take my dad fishing in Florida before December. A meaningful step I could take is to book the flights and contact a fishing guide.

## A NEW FRAMEWORK TO MINIMIZE REGRET

As mentioned, I worked for Kellogg's right out of college. While there, I earned the national salesman of the year award. It was 1997, and I was the youngest person ever to win the award. I was proud and felt like everything was going right. Three months after winning the award, I read an article in *Fast Company,* wherein Jeff Bezos talked about a concept he coined "Regret Minimization." In the interview, he described a framework to make decisions and minimize regret. For Bezos, the goal was to look back on his life with no regrets.

The article inspired me to leave my job and join a start-up. And even though it seemed like a strange move to make at the time, it was exactly the move I needed to make. It set me on a course of leaning into what I truly wanted and minimizing regret in my life. All these years later, Regret Minimization has become a philosophy by which I try to live my life. When I have difficult decisions to make, I think about what I am going to regret more—doing something, or not doing it.

Recently, a group conducted an experiment in New York City and posted the video on YouTube.[21] For the experiment, they installed a big chalkboard in the middle of Times Square that asked, *What do you regret?* For two days, people were provided with chalk to write their regrets on that board. Interestingly, 95 percent of those regrets were things people *hadn't done*, not the things they *had*. They regretted not going to law school, not having a second baby, not pursuing that career in cooking, not taking the trip to Israel.

The good news is that this kind of regret is avoidable. Every time you are faced with a big decision, you can ask yourself which course of action you will regret more: doing the thing or not doing it? If you are honest with your answer, you will know exactly what to do.

## HELL YES OR NO

You may have heard of the decision-making framework, Hell Yes or No, which was coined by entrepreneur and musician Derek Sivers and championed into the mainstream by bestselling authors Tim Ferriss and Mark Manson.[22] This simple tool is a filter for making decisions about how to spend time, energy, and money. Sivers first wrote on his blog in 2009, "If you're not feeling 'Hell yeah, that

---

[21] "What's Your Biggest Regret? (Nobody Wants to Admit the Worst One of All)," A Plus, YouTube Video, 3:25, January 25, 2016, https://www.youtube.com/watch?v=R45HcYA 8uRA.

[22] Corey Comb, "Stop Saying 'Hell Yes or No' about Your Relationships," Corey Comb, August 6, 2018, https://coreymccomb.medium.com/stop-saying-hell-yes-or-no-about-your -relationships-9b02b2d84121.

would be awesome!' about something, say no."

Anything I do now, I want to be all in. It doesn't take away from the fact that I might feel scared or nervous about it. Something might be way out of my comfort zone, and I still might be all in. This is more about asking how it makes me feel. Does it make me feel alive and full of energy? If so, count me in because I want to be excited about everything I do.

I am not always as good at this as I could be. Although the Hell Yes or No strategy is straightforward, there is often nuance involved in our decisions. It's not always easy to make that call. When I feel unsure, I try to reevaluate or pause and take additional time to think about it. In the end, if I still don't feel 100 percent up for it, I say no.

Some of the most productive times I've spent with groups, companies, and boards were focused on what they were *not* going to do. Whenever I'm working with a team of people, I collectively have them make a list. Then I ask them to decide which of the things they are going to pause. I suggest, "Let's pause what we are doing for the next three months." This is a softer delivery than saying no outright. It's more palatable for people to hear because it is not as permanent; it is just not now. People often have beliefs that they *have* to do something, but once they stop doing it they realize that it wasn't actually important or adding any value.

## The Best Leaders Say No the Most

In the beginning of a career, when you are growing a business or climbing the corporate ladder, you want to say yes to every opportunity. In those early days, saying yes can often expand your learning, stretch your comfort zone, and build your skills. Just like building a house, you need to pour the concrete first to have a solid foundation upon which you can build.

As you advance in your career, there are so many things to keep saying yes to, and sometimes it can be really hard to say no, but a large part of decision-making and scheduling your life first requires you to say no. In the book *Tribe of Mentors: Short Life Advice from the Best in the World,* Tim Ferriss explains that the most successful people say no to 90 percent of the things that are asked of them. They simply don't have the time to take advantage of every opportunity that is presented to them.

> *"People think focus means saying yes to the thing you've got to focus on. But that's not what it means at all. It means saying no to the hundred other good ideas that there are. You have to pick carefully. I'm actually as proud of the things we haven't done as the things I have done. Innovation is saying no to 1,000 things."*
>
> —STEVE JOBS

Over the years, I've realized that it can also be helpful to leave some room for spontaneity. I rarely commit to anything more than three months out. This has provided an opportunity for me to check in with myself and my energy and what I really value and what I want to do. The shadow side is that I might miss out on some opportunities. Recently, I was invited on a golf trip a year from now. I had to say no because I don't know where I'm going to be, how I am going to feel, or where my kids are going to be at that time. I start to feel anxiety planning that far in advance, which contradicts personal freedom. Some of this goes back to values. You might value lifelong learning, in which case you will prioritize new experiences that allow you to learn and grow.

## Getting the Job Done

If you're like many entrepreneurs and business leaders, you likely consider yourself a good decision maker. You make business decisions all day long, and you've learned to make better decisions along the way. But if your decisions are often focused on what's good for the company, you may not have a lot of opportunity to consider what is best for you personally.

If you're in a big company, you might not always get to use the Regret Minimization or Hell Yes or No frameworks. In these cases, you just need to make it happen and get the job done. That said, you should understand your feelings and emotions in these moments and realize that to live your best life, you want to minimize the times where you are the one who has to shift because of decisions, rather than being the one who decides.

Sometimes it's necessary to operate outside our Zone of Genius, particularly when we are early in our careers. There are jobs that have to get done that are not pleasant or rewarding. However, when we can get to more "Hell Yes" moments in our lives, we will be happier and most productive. The point is to be sure you are performing tasks in your Zone of Genius as often as possible.

## Gut Instinct in the Corporate World

There is a lot to be said for trusting your gut. When you don't feel good about a decision, explore where the uneasiness is coming from. What do you notice about the gut feeling you have when you're not sure?

When we feel like this, it's often because a decision is not aligned with our personal values. Now that you have created your personal values statement, and thought about your unique ability and Zone of Genius, you have tools to use to make sure you're making the right decisions. The next time you encounter a decision that doesn't sit quite right in your gut, ask yourself the following questions:

✓ Is it aligned with my personal values?
✓ If I'm not ready to make the decision, what do I need to make the decision?
✓ What, if anything, would change my mind? What would have to be different?
✓ What story could I tell myself that could possibly be true? If it was true, would it change my viewpoint or my decision?

Remember that if you can't get to a full-body yes, you're probably not in your Zone of Genius.

At one point during a career change, I explored starting a venture fund. In theory, it made sense and sounded very exciting, but I didn't have a full-body yes. As it got closer to pitching the idea to investors, advisors, and prospective startup companies, I felt myself hesitating. The closer it got to execution, the more I had to be realistic about how I would be spending my time. I would have to micromanage people, meet with CEOs and founders, and look at a lot of deals to make a decision about whether or not to invest in a particular company.

If I had paused, and asked whether this venture was aligned with my Zone of Genius, I would have realized it was not. Instead, I went down the path, wasting eighteen months with investors and attorneys, and making endless phone calls. I spent $35,000 in attorney fees and accountants. My initial hesitation was a red flag, and I should have paid attention. I could have saved myself a lot of time and money.

## The Pie Chart Exercise

*"Lack of direction, not lack of time is the problem.*
*We all have the same 24 hours each day."*

—ZIG ZIGLAR

Being intentional with your time means aiming to do everything consciously and on purpose. Of course nobody is perfect, but striving to live with intention each day means we are allowing only that which serves us and brings us contentment into our lives.

To be intentional with your time means being mindful of each and every task, each and every day. It is more than a one-off. It is a way of being, or at least striving for a way of being. *One way* to make sure you are prioritizing your life based on your values and Zone of Genius is by looking at where you spend your time:

1. Draw a pie chart.
2. Fill the pie chart with an estimate of how you spend your time today.

For example, in a day, you might spend eight hours, or roughly 34 percent, sleeping. Ten hours at work equates to 41 percent; one hour getting ready for work; one and a half hours commuting; one hour exercising. This leaves an hour and a half with your family—dinner and bedtime, and one hour to watch TV or scroll your phone.

Now think about how much time you spent outdoors in a week: _____%

1. Now draw a second pie chart: Aspirationally, where should you be spending your time based on your values and your Zone of Genius. In a year, how do you want your pie chart to look?
2. What do you need to change in your life to make that happen?
   a. What's in the way?
   b. What can help you prioritize more effectively?

Being intentional with your time means holding yourself accountable every day for the choices and decisions you make. You will need to focus every day to be mindful of how you are living.

## The Seven-Seven-Seven Exercise

The creative exercise of writing your own eulogy was popularized by Michael Hyatt and Daniel Harkavy, the authors of *Living*

*Forward: A Proven Plan to Stop Drifting and Get the Life You Want.*
The intent of this exercise is to help you consider the life you want
to be leading.

I found a different exercise that distills time so clearly that it
motivates me into action and helps me remember that change can
happen in a moment. I encourage you to try it out. *Imagine you have
seven years left to live. How are you going to spend your time? Write
those things down.*

If I had seven years to live, I would want to go on a safari. I would
want to see my kids graduate from college. And I would probably
work less. But, for the most part, I am pleased to say I wouldn't do
much differently. I have been fortunate to craft a life around my
personal values statement and Zone of Genius. If this is not your
current situation, now is your opportunity to create your future.

Next step: *Imagine that something changed and you only have seven
months to live; how are you going to spend your time now? Write those
things down.*

Seven months is a little different than seven years. In seven
months, I would want to get my finances in order and make sure
that Aly is taken care of. We would have conversations about a will
and trusts. I would probably record some videos for my kids. I would
like to leave a video for them to watch at their life milestones, such
as college graduation and when they have their first child, to tell
them how proud I am of them. I would spend all the time I could
with my family, and I probably wouldn't work at all.

Final step: *Now, imagine the doctor revised your prognosis and gave
you seven days left to live. How are you going to spend your time?*

Shit, seven days. The kids would not go to school. I wouldn't tell them when to go to bed. We would just stay up all night and talk. I would just want to spend time with them. I would make a list of all of the friends who have given me energy and supported me over my life. I would probably hike a mountain and sit at the peak, spending the day making phone calls to those people, taking what time I had left to tell them how grateful I am for them.

By doing this exercise, you see what is most important in your life. For me, everything distilled down to time with Aly and the kids. This aligns with my personal values and how I already prioritize my life. This is a way I can know my values and actions are aligned, and not only showing up if I have only a little time left to live.

This exercise might provide clarity for you as well. I recommend doing it at least once every year, and revisiting your answers quarterly.

## Moments That Shape Us

In December 2013, I was attending a conference in Palm Beach, and Aly and I decided to make a short getaway out of the trip. We were having breakfast on a main street patio and, as I was getting ready to pay the bill, I looked up to see a bald, shirtless man on his morning run.

It was Jeff Bezos.

"This is your chance to meet him! Let's go!" Aly said.

I really wanted to, but my own sense of decorum got in the way; I was just too embarrassed. *Oh come on, am I really going to stalk Jeff Bezos while he is running?* I wondered. But Aly was persistent. "Come on, we're going. Get in the car!"

I started to get excited. There we were, driving slowly down Florida Scenic Highway A1A trying to orchestrate a chance meeting with Jeff Bezos. We could see him about a half mile ahead, two or three stoplights away. We saw him turn the corner and I remember saying to myself, *I bet he's staying at The Breakers*, which is one of the nicest hotels in Palm Beach, a historic luxury oceanfront resort. There is a long, opulent garden at the entrance, with a guard shack and gate. Beyond the gate, there is a lushly landscaped thousand-foot front drive.

As we waited at the stoplight, I spotted him standing just to the side of the main driveway of the hotel. As we turned in, Aly said, "I think you've got to get out of the car and make up a story at the guard shack." With that, she pushed me out of the car.

Aly is not normally like this, but she knew what it would mean to me to have a chance to meet Jeff Bezos. Although I didn't realize it at the time, she was practicing Regret Minimization on my behalf; had I not spoken to him, I would have regretted it for the rest of my life.

This was it, the moment of truth. I could see his bald head through the bushes. His run was over, and he was heading into the lobby. I shimmied through the bushes until I was right behind him. I started walking almost step-for-step, three steps behind him, to his left, and then increased my pace until I was alongside him. And then I waited as we walked next to each other for twenty or thirty yards.

Finally, I looked over as casually as I possibly could and said, "Oh, hey Jeff, I'm Bart Foster." But I kept walking. I didn't make a point of trying to stop him because I knew he probably got that all the time. I left some space as if we were just two guests going to the pool. I said,

"You know, I wanted to share with you, you've made a big impact on my life." He kept walking, so I got more specific. "In 1997, I read an article in *Fast Company*. You said that the reason you moved from New York to start Amazon was due to Regret Minimization."

At this point, he stopped, turned to face me, and smiled. "What's your name again?" he asked. "Tell me about your business. What do you do? Who are you?"

We kept walking to the pool, and I told him about SoloHealth. He wanted to know about the future of healthcare and my perspective on self-service medical care. He also cautioned me about having too much of my business with Walmart. After six or seven minutes, we parted ways.

It was a full-circle moment to have run into Jeff sixteen years after reading the article—which shaped who I became and set me along a completely different path.

As you grow in prioritizing your life through Regret Minimization and more Hell Yeses, you will be able to look back and realize just how important these steps were in your life. It's not always easy to see how far an aligned decision can take you, but it might just lead you to a chance encounter with one of your heroes.

# CHAPTER TEN

# Anchors and Rockets

*"A ship in harbor is safe, but that's not*
*what ships are built for."*

—JOHN SHEDD

IN THE SPRING OF 2014, I GOT A CALL FROM MY CHAIRMAN, LARRY, asking me if I wanted to go to breakfast that weekend. We decided to meet at the Flying Biscuit in the north side of Atlanta. When I walked in, Larry was already seated at a table. Tall and broad-shouldered, he was a presence, and had a congenial, Midwestern charm about him.

Larry was a good friend of my uncle's and had provided capital for SoloHealth when the market tanked in 2008. I had quickly asked him to be the chairman of the board, knowing his experience and credibility would be an asset. For six years, he provided direction and served a prominent role in attracting investors to help scale our business. I felt proud and excited that we were able to raise $50 million in funding together.

Over breakfast, Larry and I exchanged pleasantries, and then he asked me, "How big do you want this company to get?"

As CEO of SoloHealth, I had thrived by inspiring and empowering an expanding staff and creating a nurturing work culture that grew and grew. With Larry's help connecting me to investors, I had grown the business into a high-growth success story with a national footprint, impacting more than 50 million people. All of this meant a lot to me.

I gave Larry a number in response to his question. "Oh, I think the company is worth that today," he replied. "But every once in a while, I run across a business that has all the makings of going public. And I think this is one of those situations."

I was intrigued and excited.

"I've taken three companies public and have a lot of experience," Larry continued. "I think we should go a lot bigger, Bart. But we would have to make a few changes."

Feeling exhilarated about this prospect, I jumped right in, explaining the changes I thought we would have to make if we were to go public. I knew we would need to upgrade some of our management team. We would probably need a different CFO, too. As it turned out, I wasn't quite picking up what Larry was putting down.

He leaned back in his chair and said, "Bart, I would even consider being CEO for a while."

Suddenly the casual nature of this breakfast conversation seemed to shift. My stomach lurched, and my heart started beating faster. I felt a range of emotions, running the gamut from confusion to anger to betrayal. This right here was my biggest fear. *I* was the CEO. Was I being forced out of the company I had founded?

"What do you mean?" I asked Larry.

"Oh, you know," he said. "I'd come in as CEO for a while, and you could take whatever position you want. Maybe Head of Strategy. We can work that out. But I don't want to do it unless you're fully on board, so why don't you think about it over the weekend? You might want to talk to your wife."

It was starting to sink in.

I got back in the car and cried the whole way back to the office. Thinking Larry had gone behind my back, I called the other board members on the way home. They assured me my place in the company was safe. "No, no, you're the CEO," they told me. "We'll talk to Larry. Maybe he's bored and needs something to do." We agreed to give him a role, to put him in finance and have him raise capital because that's where he could best add value.

It was settled, or so I thought.

On Monday morning, Larry strode into the office wearing a three-piece suit. As an early-stage start-up, our culture was laid back and we wore what we wanted. Larry looked out-of-place, but it was clear he meant business. I had known he was coming in, so I scheduled a meeting in the boardroom with my executive team. Out of respect, I gave Larry the seat at the head of the table. Everyone in the company knew him, so I started the meeting by saying, "I'm excited to announce that you'll be seeing Larry around the office a lot more because he's going to be joining us as the Executive Chairman. I'm really proud of where we've taken this company so far, and now Larry's going to help us take it to the next level."

I'll never forget what happened next.

"Well, guys," Larry said, "I've got to commend Bart for stepping aside. We've got a lot of work to do."

I didn't hear anything after that. That's the moment I realized one very important thing: when you raise $50 million in capital, it's not your company anymore. As Executive Chairman, Larry now had the authority to hire and fire. He started making decisions that were clearly my decisions to make and started usurping everything. Soon enough, it felt like there were two CEOs, and I knew that was not going to work at all.

The concept of anchors and rockets is straightforward: anchors hold us back, while rockets propel us forward. There are many anchors and rockets in your life: people, processes, a core belief, fear, geography, a job, a book, time, money, opportunities, and resources, just to start. And a single thing might serve as both an anchor *and* a rocket at different times in your life. Larry served as a rocket in the early days of SoloHealth, and then as an anchor when this shift occurred.

In this chapter, we will identify the anchors holding you back and the rockets that can accelerate your growth.

 **ANCHORS**

In nautical terms, an anchor is used to prevent a vessel from drifting away in the wind or current. An anchorman or anchorwoman on broadcast news provides continuity, a familiar face, and establishes trust. As a negotiating technique, setting the anchor establishes a reference point around which a negotiation will revolve. The anchor will often be used as a reference point to make adjustments and often occurs when the first offer is presented at the beginning of a negotiation. This is all to say that anchors have their place; they can be helpful when we need something to be tethered down, literally or figuratively.

But anchors can also hold you back. It's important to be able to locate anchors in your life and have an antidote for them. The only way to see the opportunities life has in store for you is to cut the anchor and set sail. It's generally not possible to simultaneously remain in the safety of the harbor and crush your goals.

## Five-Star Relationships

If a person is holding you back, they are an anchor. I saw this first-hand while working with one of my coaching clients, Carla, whose longtime boyfriend was taking a lot of her energy. I walked her through an exercise to help her get clarity on what she wanted. "Forget this guy for a second," I said. "What are the most important attributes in a relationship? If you could wave a magic wand, what would your relationship look like?" I took out a notebook and wrote down her responses.

She listed roughly twenty relationship attributes that were most important to her, such as: interesting to talk to, adventurous, curious, hardworking, spontaneous, healthy, energetic. Next, I had her rank how frequently she saw those attributes in her partner, in the past six months, on a scale of one to five with one being never and five being always. How much did they exude or live into those attributes? Her list included only two fives.

I looked at Carla and said, "Don't settle. Find somebody who is all fours and fives. Go make it happen."

And she did.

That was a turning point for Carla: she realized that to be the best version of herself, and the happiest, she needed to start looking for someone in her life who had a larger percentage of those attributes. When we are in a relationship with someone who is an anchor, they hold us back from being the best we can be. In contrast, if we spend time with people who give us energy, who make us better, we can accelerate our happiness. Carla found a new partner who made her better. She took control of her life by being more intentional with what she wanted and then went and found it. She now is happier, healthier, and more confident.

# Fear

People are not the only anchors. Fear is one of the biggest anchors, and shows up in different ways for different people, such as fear of failure, lack of confidence, or fear of not belonging. Sometimes fear doesn't even look like fear; instead it may present itself as a feeling of unworthiness, imposter syndrome, paralysis, or inaction. Unless you break through fear, it can weigh you down and keep you from realizing your full potential.

After working with thousands of executives, I have identified the five most common fears people struggle with.

## 1. Fear of failure.

When you are afraid to fail, you are less likely to take a risk, missing the opportunity to expand that circle of comfort. You reject the opportunity for growth and advancement because it opens you up to the possibility of failing. Recently, I was listening to a performer talk about juggling. "The only way we can be a good juggler is by being willing to drop the ball," he explained. You have to practice. Dropping the ball is part of what helps you learn. This is the opposite of what we were taught in school.

Lean into the willingness to fail. Your fear of failure may be keeping you in that same role, even though you don't have anything left to learn. Or you might not go for it with the business idea you've had for a long time because you're afraid you might fail.

A fear of failing publicly, and of the consequences, could prevent you from making a conscious choice and taking a conscious action.

Take action regardless of the outcome. If you want to get that pro-motion, start your own company, change careers, or have a different life, you have to accept that risk is part of the package. It's trite but true: *nothing ventured, nothing gained.* To succeed, you must have the ability to take risks, the willingness to be fired, and the courage to live with uncertainty.

## 2. Lack of confidence.

If you lack confidence, you are going to have trouble connecting with other people and asking for what you really want, instead of passively waiting for things to be handed to you. That might include a pro-motion, a new role, or a thriving relationship, among other things.

Some people think that if they just keep working hard, their boss is eventually going to notice and give them a raise. We tell ourselves a story about how if we're nice and compliant, and do what we're supposed to do, others will want to do business with us. But it's by connecting with other people, articulating your own value and your own Zone of Genius, and confidently asking for what you want that will move you forward.

Lack of confidence can sometimes stem from feeling unworthy or undeserving of what you have. Some people conflate being self-deprecating with being humble, but it's not the same. It might seem innocent to brush off a compliment or make a joke about yourself, but what you're actually doing is putting yourself down. Over time, this negative self-talk can reinforce an idea of unworthiness or that you don't deserve any number of things you've earned, including awards, accolades, praise, and compliments.

If you feel unworthy of what you've already been given, you're going to shy away from opportunities to expand, making it harder to achieve your goals. Instead, own your contribution to the world. Lean into your Zone of Genius. Knowing that my Zone of Genius can make a difference for another person has helped me with both my confidence and my worth. When I connect with somebody, I often think about reciprocity: What can I give back? What are my unique skills and how can I give them something of value?

Oftentimes people have the competence; they just don't demonstrate it because they fear judgment or the possibility of being inadequate. Those feelings might manifest as not expressing an important opinion or expressing it without conviction.

### 3. Imposter syndrome.

If you feel held back by an intense fear that people are going to find out you are a fake, you run the risk of disallowing others to get too close. You fear that if they spend too much time with you, they are going to discover the truth: that you are not as talented, smart, creative, innovative, or imaginative as you've made yourself out to be.

I've had this experience several times in my career. As a CEO, I thought I had to be great at reading a P&L statement and proficient at reviewing annual reports of public companies. I was often worried people were going to figure me out.

But there's a positive side to imposter syndrome: it keeps you learning and growing. As Adam Grant explains in his book *Think Again*, imposter syndrome can motivate you to work harder, work smarter, and be a better learner. Here's a secret: We all experience "imposter syndrome" at some point. Learn to make it work for you. After all, we're all just figuring this out. Everyone is so busy starring in their own movie that no one is watching yours.

## 4. Fear of judgment.

People tend to judge others based upon their own core values and insecurities, but values and insecurities differ from person to person. In the end, it's almost impossible to escape judgment.

To combat fear of judgment, you need to be clear about who you are and not worry about what others think. The problem with caring about what other people think is that over time you start to let other people define who you are. If you have done the work in Chapters Three and Four, you are clear on your core values and what is important to you. You know who you are, so take back the power you have allowed other people to take from you. When your anxiety alarms the "What if's" like "What if they think I'm mean?" I challenge you to ask yourself if being mean is how you define yourself. If not, forget that internal dialogue; you know your intentions. When you're clear on who you are and your intentions, you can focus on what you're trying to accomplish—and on the big picture.

Finally, remember that people don't care. A study done by the National Science Foundation claims that people have, on average, 50,000 plus thoughts a day. This means that even if someone thought about us ten times in one day, it's only 0.2 percent of their overall daily thoughts. It's a sad but simple truth that the average person filters their world through their ego, meaning that they think of most things relating to "me" or "my." Unless you've done something that directly affects another person or their life, they are not going to spend much time thinking about you at all.

If you're still struggling with fear of judgment, I encourage you to take a look at Sean Kim's article on lifehacker, titled "How to Stop Giving a F**k What People Think."[23]

## 5. Inability to take action.

Some people are held back by their inability to get out of their own way. They become overwhelmed by change, whether it be starting a new career, taking the entrepreneurial route, accepting a new job, or anything else. They look at the mountain of decisions they have to make, shut down, and end up not doing anything.

People who suffer from the inability to take action are deferring responsibility or refusing to make a decision, but they are still making a conscious choice by choosing to do nothing about the current situation.

Inaction and paralysis are not going to move you closer to what you want to achieve. If you are telling yourself you want to live a better life, get a different job, change careers, or move into a different relationship, you'll have to take intentional action steps. You can't do nothing and hope things work out. As author Rick Page said, "Hope is not a strategy." Start cultivating a bias for action. Start building that muscle. Every time you want to stay still or step back, lean in instead. Have a bias for action.

---

[23] Sean Kim, "How to Stop Giving a F*ck What People Think," Lifehacker, February 25, 2014, https://lifehacker.com/how-to-stop-giving-a-f-ck-what-people-think-1530784365.

## Removing the Anchor

No matter which anchor is holding you back, it's important to recognize that you're living with a false belief. Whether it's fear of failure, fear of success, fear of judgment, or imposter syndrome, the anchor and the false belief are keeping you small—keeping you from playing full out and living a bigger life. It's time to remove the anchors, eliminate the barriers holding you back, and tell a new story. Here is a way to begin that process:

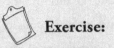

### Exercise:
### Identify the Anchors in Your Life

In the previous chapters, you assessed your personal values and Zone of Genius on a scale of one to five, with how often you are living that particular value, or are in your Zone of Genius, in the previous six months. One was "Never" and five was "Always."

Review anything you ranked a three or lower, and then take some time to consider the anchors that might be keeping you at that number. What is holding you back? Write down your answers and then return to the exercise outlined in Chapter Eight for moving through false beliefs.

 **ROCKETS**

For many years, rockets launching into orbit used 84.3 percent of the total fuel for the trip in the first three minutes. That might sound crazy, but it was the standard. Today, the spacecrafts being developed by SpaceX use only a fraction of that percentage to get to space. The Falcon 9, for example, used only 8 percent of the amount of fuel that the first Apollo mission used. Space travel technology is getting better, faster, and leaner. So, too, is our understanding of how to accelerate our personal growth.

For the person trying to live a more intentional life, there are many ways to reach orbit that don't involve burning through your rocket fuel in the first three minutes.

## Abundance Mindset

Having an abundance mindset is an excellent way to reach orbit faster and more efficiently.

People with a scarcity mindset focus on unfulfilled needs, and what others have that they don't. They tend to think in the short-term and have relationships that are less fulfilling. Those with an abundance mindset focus on what they already have and make peace with the present moment because they are not living in a state of fear. They experience gratitude, make better decisions, and plan for the future.

Signs that you have an abundance mindset:

- **You celebrate other people's success.** This is the opposite of jealousy and fear. You believe that other people's success is not going to detract from your own.
- **You give back.** Those stuck in a scarcity mindset are too busy taking things from other people to give back. In an abundance mindset, you care about people and therefore volunteer your time, energy, and skills.
- **You live in the present moment.** If you focus on gratitude in abundance, you're not worried about the future and you don't get stuck in the past. You know that the only thing that is guaranteed is right here in the present moment. You are able to focus and take it all in.

### Developing an Abundance Mindset

Examine your limiting beliefs. During our interview, Erin Pheil defined limiting beliefs as unconscious beliefs that we hold about ourselves and the world that prevent us from enjoying our lives to the fullest. Identifying these unconscious beliefs doesn't come easy, even under the best circumstances.

One of the most effective practices I've used to wake up from my unconscious patterns is the practice of gratitude. This doesn't have to be complicated. I like to simply make a list of all of the things I am grateful for. If you embrace this process of cultivating gratitude in your life, you will be able to better spot limiting beliefs and examine how they are preventing you from reaching your full potential. You'll give yourself space to adopt empowering beliefs. And you'll be able to flip limiting beliefs by asking yourself: does this belief take me further along in the pursuit of gratitude or does it hold me back?

In life, our mindset determines which path we travel on. One path is paved in scarcity and the other is paved in abundance. At any moment, we can choose to change which path we want to travel on. The scarcity path leads to an experience of a life that is not fulfilled, one that can only be described as mundane or pedestrian. This life is overflowing with strong, negative reactions and missed opportunities.

By choosing to walk down that abundance path, we get to experience a completely different life. We are opting to live life to the fullest. We're happier, and by nature, we are generous, creative, and inspirational. We take full advantage of all the opportunities that come our way. We believe there is plenty of everything for everybody in the world, and this changes our approach to everything.

## Increasing Efficiency

Money is one of the biggest accelerants, and the lack of it can act as an anchor. Ramit Sethi, a personal finance advisor and author of *I Will Teach You to Be Rich,* shares that many of us learn how to save money, but rarely do we know how to *spend* money. If you are a person with even some means, you can utilize money to make your life easier or more efficient and eliminate friction points.

I have recently been experimenting more with new ways to spend my money in order to increase efficiency in my life. For example, when I am leading a workshop, I now bring in a second facilitator so I am freed up to develop more relationships, read the room, and have time to think. With this "investment," I have the space to have sidebar conversations between sessions, and at least some of these inevitably lead to more business down the line. I also now bring in a graphic recorder, who uses words and pictures to capture the meeting's key takeaways. This makes the event run smoother and provides value for the participants. I even hired an intern earlier this year who is a total rocket. He has unlimited potential and takes everything I throw at him with enthusiasm, including data entry, graphic design, social media, and some of the more mundane tasks that I hate doing, freeing me up to do other things.

For so long, I would do all of these tasks myself because I could knock them out quickly and wanted to keep the revenue. Sethi's philosophy, which is based on an abundance mindset, helped me realize that offloading these tasks to people who are working in *their* Zone of Genius—and, therefore, better and more efficient at doing them—makes my business run more smoothly and efficiently. Although my short-term cash flow for that particular project might be lower, I'm freed up to bring in more business, and to do things more aligned with my personal values and Zone of Genius. In several cases, I've ended up getting additional gigs simply because I've had the time to enjoy dinner conversations and was not completely spent from leading sessions all day.

Hiking offers a great metaphor for spending resources wisely. On trail, you use a switchback to ease the journey. Instead of hiking straight up the mountain, you traverse back and forth with a less steep grade. The trek might take longer than it would if you went straight up the mountain, but it also makes it doable. You can use the same philosophy in life. You might need to pay more money, time, or energy up-front, but that investment will make the journey more enjoyable, and you'll reach the summit with energy left in the tank.

## People as Rockets

For me, people are often my biggest rockets: mentors, friends, colleagues, family, advisors, board members, colleagues. Who are the people in your own life that will take you further?

As I mentioned in Chapter Three, when I was in my early twenties I read *Dig Your Well Before You're Thirsty* by Harvey Mackay. That book was a powerful rocket for me because it provided a path to building and cultivating relationships with people all over the world, who in turn became rockets for me.

I currently have a list of eighteen people who I call my "energy enhancers." They are my rockets; they give me confidence, make me stronger, get me out of my comfort zone, make me smile, bring me joy, give me fuel.

Some rockets in our lives are super connectors: they know a lot of people across multiple industries and disciplines, and have relationships all over the world that could be the rocket fuel you are missing.

Others are rockets for a period of time, and then turn into an anchor, or vice versa. Human relationships are complex and they evolve.

Some people can also be rockets and anchors at the same time. They inspire you, but with them you can only move so fast. Children can be like this. They give you motivation to lead by example. You may be driven to be successful for them, or to be a great parent. At the same time, you have to move a little slower when you have kids, especially little kids. This is a simple reality of life.

## Turning Anchors into Rockets

It's important to recognize that anchors do not have to stay anchors. In fact, they can become some of the biggest rockets in your life. For example, you might have a board member who is prickly, opposes what you want to do, or is adversarial because you didn't take the time to develop the relationship. If you take the time to cultivate that relationship, understand where they are coming from, seek to have empathy, and spend time to help them see your perspective, they can become your biggest support. They can open up new doors, or a new pathway to funding.

The most important thing is to assess your relationships with the people around you on a regular basis. How do you feel about a certain person? Do they give you energy, or are they zapping it? Are their beliefs and judgments serving you or not? When you sense someone may be an anchor in your life, you need to assess: *should I work to change this, perhaps by clearing an issue (as explained in Chapter Three), or do I need to remove them from my life entirely?*

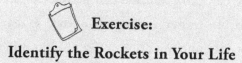 **Exercise:**

## Identify the Rockets in Your Life

What are the assets, tools, resources, and people who could accelerate your growth? Use the Make it Happen Worksheet in the Appendix to write a list of the potential rockets and energy enhancers and then consider how to leverage these rockets. For example, a strong mentor can open doors and guide you to places you would have never dreamed. They could accelerate your growth by providing wisdom and advice, saving time and money.

## Reaching Orbit

Larry is still running the company I founded and at the time of printing, has yet to take the company public. After that day in the boardroom where Larry commended me for "stepping aside," I agreed to become the Head of Strategy but quickly realized things weren't working in this new setup. There were two people trying to lead with different visions. So, three months later I left. I stayed on the Board for a couple of years before eventually realizing that it was best for me, emotionally and mentally, to resign. I sold all my shares and was able to use that to build my next business venture.

I was on a hike recently and someone asked me what the best gift was I have ever been given? The immediate thing that came to mind was the day Larry told me that he wanted to be CEO. My eventual departure from the company opened so many doors and allowed me to lean into my Zone of Genius. It provided a shock to the system that I didn't know I needed.

I began assessing my life and started asking questions again. *What is really important in life? What do I really value and who do I want to spend my time with? Am I leveraging my unique gifts and abilities?* I didn't realize it at the time, but that adversity forced me to expand my circle of comfort and experience the supreme discomfort that comes with growth. It truly was a gift.

My biggest lesson was realizing that so much of my personal identity was tied up in SoloHealth. And that really wasn't who I was. That was a *piece* of who I was, certainly, and it was something I was proud to have created, but I am so much more than just a company and the CEO title. What matters more is who I am as a person. After that point, things began to crystallize for me: when I leverage my Zone of Genius and lean into my personal values, that's when I am happiest.

I was intentional with the way I crafted my life once I started down this path. What I do now with BusinessOutside feels like all the best parts of being a CEO without all the things I am not good at: finance, logistics, operations, hiring, and human resources.

My kids get to see firsthand how I went through adversity, came out the other side, and am now happier and healthier. I am leaning into my personal values statement, living and working with personal freedom. It allows me to live an active and healthy life full of adventure.

The summer after that pivotal moment in my company, I took off to travel with my family and to discover my identity without the CEO title. By taking the time to reflect on what I had learned over the past ten years instead of focusing on how to leverage my success for the future, I found the courage to let go of my ego. I reconnected with friends and family I hadn't seen in years and engaged in deep and meaningful discussions with my wife, reflecting on what was most important to us.

Our move to Boulder was a direct result of my departure from SoloHealth. I didn't know it eight years ago, but I was already doing business outside. I didn't have that concept, it wasn't a name, but I was definitely operating outside of my comfort zone. I left a very comfortable life in the suburbs of Atlanta to rebuild a life in Boulder, which is much more suited to who I am. The social scene here in Boulder is not material-driven. No one cares what car you drive or what brand of clothes you wear. They are interested in how many sunrises you saw last week or what marathon you might be training for next. Life here is more centered around life experiences, which aligns with my personal values. When people ask, "What do you do here?" they really just want to know if you mountain bike or ski? They don't really care what you do for a living. These are my people. And it took my experience with Larry to get me here.

It's true. Sometimes the most unlikely sources—even anchors— will ultimately lead us into orbit.

# CHAPTER ELEVEN

# Accelerate the Inevitable

*"You can either delay or speed up the inevitable;*
*but you cannot prevent it from staying the course."*

—JOAN AMBU

Elon Musk, the richest man in the world, was speaking at Stanford Business School a few years ago about his thoughts on Tesla, SolarCity, and SpaceX.[24] At the end of his talk, he was asked how he came up with ideas for what to work on next. He responded by telling two quick stories, the first about how he was sitting on a tractor at twenty years old when he looked down and suddenly understood we were not going to have combustion engines forever. "This is an inevitable fact," he said. "We are going to have electric cars." Elon believed long before anyone else that electro-transportation was not just a possibility for our future but an inevitability. Two years later, he was looking up at the moon and thought, "Since we have already been to the moon, going to Mars is inevitable."

Musk went on to say that he has dedicated his life to having everything he works on "accelerate the inevitable." He has indeed moved an entire industry forward, to fundamentally change the way we act and behave.

I started taking this concept and applying it in my own work with clients. I recently led an event that gathered eye care executives from around the world and brought them into the same room together. I asked them to consider what would absolutely happen in the eye care industry, without question, in the next five to seven years? Everyone brainstormed and shared their thoughts about the future of eye care. Responses included things like the arrival of remote refraction, telemedicine, and continued consolidation by

---

[24] David Cummings, "Video of the Week: Elon Musk at Stanford GSB," David Cummings on Startup, January 29, 2016, https://davidcummings.org/2016/01/29/video-of-the-week-elon-musk-at-stanford-gsb/.

private equity firms. In no time, we had a Top 10 list of what was definitely going to happen in the future of eye care. Details such as who was going to do it or when it would happen were irrelevant; we were simply focusing on the *inevitable*.

You can apply this concept in any industry and in your personal life, too, if you want to think differently—without the constraints of money, time, and execution. Once you have identified the inevitable, you have three options: (1) you can either wait to see what happens, (2) you can try to slow it down, or (3) you can lean in and *accelerate the inevitable*. Nothing leads to an intentional life more than becoming an accelerant.

## THE BOLD PATH VS. THE PREDICTABLE PATH

There are inevitabilities in every industry. Uber accelerated the transportation industry; Netflix accelerated the entertainment industry; Airbnb accelerated the lodging industry. In the eye care industry, Warby Parker identified the inevitability that consumers would get tired of spending $400 on a pair of glasses. When they found out the eyewear industry is dominated by a single company that has been able to keep prices artificially high while reaping huge profits from consumers with no other options, Warby Parker cut out the middleman and cut costs by 75 percent. They accelerated the inevitable.

When I was at Novartis and thought of creating a vision screening kiosk, the idea felt inevitable to me; consumers would begin screening their own vision at some point down the line. At the time, most people in the eye care industry weren't quite ready for the idea of having a device that allowed someone to test their own vision. I got struck down by regulatory constraints, big associations, and lobby groups that wanted to protect their profession. In 2021, Warby Parker contacted me to consult with them about creating—you guessed it!—a vision-screening kiosk. The idea is likely going to come full circle. The lesson here is that you can't always predict the time it will take to bring the inevitable into being, but you can take the first steps to be ahead of the curve and a leader in your industry.

## THE PANDEMIC AFFECTED THE WAY WE WORK

The way people work was upended during the pandemic, and accelerated the inevitability of people realizing there is more to life than the nine-to-five grind. The traditional work day in corporate America got a shake-up. The lockdown was the perfect opportunity for corporations and employees alike to evaluate whether or not they wanted to continue doing things the same way they always had.

Commercial real estate was affected as people moved out of big cities and sought out nature. Workers began trying to get out of urban spaces because they had gotten used to not having to commute and realized they can do good work from anywhere. Suddenly, employees were getting back the ten hours a week they used to spend commuting. Now they could do more things they loved: more sleep, more time outdoors, more time with family, more time for hobbies. For many employees, quality of life improved.

It was inevitable that we were going to be more digitally connected and partake in more video calls. Without the COVID-19 lockdown, it likely would have taken another eight to ten years for this to happen, but the pandemic accelerated this inevitability.

At the same time, with less of a separation between home life and work life and more time spent sitting in front of a computer, people have forgotten how to socialize. People rely on their devices more than at any other time in history and screen time has skyrocketed.

As a byproduct of circumstances, corporations have had to accelerate their thinking about the workplace and work environment. New questions are being asked. *What does it mean to go to work? Does the open office plan work? Do offices with a door and C-Suite work, or do we need to rethink everything?*

I would argue that we have to rethink everything. Two years into the pandemic, companies are trying to adapt to the ever-changing situation, looking at back-to-the office plans to figure out how to entice employees back to the physical office space, or whether they even should.

All of this reassessment and recalibration wipes away that stagnation and forces us to adapt, similar to the way a forest fire clears the weaker trees and debris and returns health to the forest. This kind of shake-up brings a fresh perspective. It also brings a resilience that will be useful the next time there's a bump in the road.

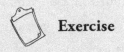

**Exercise**

1. Think deeply about what is inevitable in your business, and your industry.
2. Think deeply about what is inevitable in your personal life.
3. Write these down clearly and concisely.
4. What would happen if you helped accelerate this change?

BusinessOutside is all about leaning into the inevitable, and I invite you to come along for the ride. It's incredibly empowering to help drive the future.

CHAPTER TWELVE

# Make It Happen

> "*The distance between dreams and reality is called action.*"
>
> —BEN FRANCIA

THROUGHOUT THIS BOOK, I HAVE ASKED YOU TO CONSIDER WHAT you really want to do with your life. I encouraged you to get clarity on your personal values and craft a statement that means something to you. Then you identified your Zone of Genius. Both of these together create a strong foundation from which the rest of your life can flow. In this chapter, we will look at how to take steps forward and make things happen.

What have you been dreaming about but not taking action on? People make a lot of excuses about why they can't do something when really, they can. *You can.* You can find a way. I promise. You just have to eliminate the obstacles and take one step at a time.

I have helped many of my clients shape their career, and I have seen over and over that the ones who actually take charge and make their vision for their life happen have been able to shape an entirely new life for themselves. Of course, the path forward is not always clear.

I remember working with one client who had already gone through years of school when we met. It appeared that his course in life was already set. There was just one problem: he didn't actually want to be a lawyer.

When I asked him what he loved to do and what he was great at, he explained how he loves to make things with his hands, but he was concerned that something like carpentry wouldn't pay the bills. So, we started with a first step. I asked him to identify one step he could take to make it happen. It could be as simple as spending time on the weekends living in his passion. Did he have a workspace set up, say in his garage? If not, that would be an action he could take. Did he have the correct tools and equipment? If not, he could go out and buy some.

Taking that first step led him to the next right action, and he is now a thriving carpenter making custom dining room pieces for customers across the country. Remember that you don't have to make your passion support you financially, especially when first starting. But if you want to make a living in your Zone of Genius, it's important to take the first steps to build up to that.

One way to take that first step is to go to a place where others are already doing what you want and volunteer. The point is to get in the garage, get the tools, start doing what you love more often. Just remember that in order to take these steps, you'll need some discipline. You might need to start waking up earlier, watching less TV, and scrolling your phone less. But as you carve out more and more time in your life, you'll find the space and energy to develop your passion.

Amazing things happen when you take steps toward what you really want in life. Soon enough, you might find you're doing everything you dreamed of.

This was certainly true for my friend, Karen, who was a teacher and wanted to become a writer. She knew she needed to take first steps forward to make it happen, so she started writing articles for her local newspaper. It didn't pay, but the connections she made with editors allowed her to start writing for other publications. She was "paid" by getting tickets to concerts, events, plays, and festivals in her community. She got to do all kinds of fun stuff around town and learn her craft at the same time.

Within a few months, she started getting paid to write blogs, was hired on retainer to write articles for an online publication, and ultimately got a book deal with a publisher. She had started writing for free in January and had a book deal by July. Twelve years later, she is still living in her Zone of Genius. She took the leap first without knowing how it was going to work, and everything fell easily into place from there.

You can have a story like this, too, but you have to get started. An excellent first step is to talk to as many people as you can who are doing what you want to do; find out how they got into the field and ask if they have any advice. Simply have those conversations. Ask questions, ask for tips, ask if they would be willing to mentor you. And when you have some answers, take the next step. It's simple, but few are willing to actually put in the effort.

## CURRENT REALITY TO FUTURE REALITY

Lita Currie, a graphic recorder I work with, posted something on LinkedIn recently that perfectly illustrates the concept of making things happen and changing your life.

"When I was in the process of making the decision to leave corporate," she writes in her post, "I created a current and future reality visual to help me decide on three bold actions to move forward. Four years later, it's fascinating to see what I have achieved."

Today, Lita no longer has to do annual budgets, be on the clock, or have performance reviews and endless meetings. She achieved her goal by taking three action steps:

- Built her network
- Completed a coaching qualification
- Registered a business

Her future reality included: facilitation, collaboration, cake decorating, and four vacations a year. Four years later, she is doing work that gives her energy—facilitation, graphic recording, and collaborating with amazing people. She is spending time on the things that are important to her.

I encourage you to take a few minutes to create your own Current Reality → Future Reality. What do you want to leave behind? Where do you want to go? In order to get there, what are three specific actions you can take?

## THE POWER OF RITUALS

It can feel overwhelming to create a future reality. One of the most effective ways I have been able to make change happen in my life has been through rituals. I define rituals as a series of actions taken towards a specific goal. By outlining rituals for yourself, you can start taking action right away.

Here is an example:

> **Ritual and Reason:** Disconnect from technology when I get home from work. This will allow me to be fully present with my family.
>
> **Frequency:** I want to do this three times a week.
>
> **Partners:** The people who are going to hold me accountable are my wife and the kids, and a close colleague.
>
> Note that having an accountability partner always helps with follow-through and results. If I check in every Sunday with an accountability partner, I'm much more likely to stick with a ritual.

## CREATING YOUR NEW STORY

You *can* re-craft the story of your life. Your current "old" story is the mindset that has prevented personal growth, made you a victim of your circumstances, and blocked you from achieving your full happiness. Your "new story" is the one that realigns your energy with your purpose. By changing your story, you are choosing to shift to a growth mindset and move past your limiting beliefs.

For example, my old story was that I was forced out of the company I founded. The new story I choose to focus on is how I was able to create a business that impacted millions of people. In my early days at SoloHealth, I was in my Zone of Genius, developing the first self-service health kiosks and ultimately getting them into over four thousand locations. As the company grew, I realized I was no longer operating in my Zone of Genius and eventually knew it was time to move on. By telling a new story about my experience at SoloHealth and beyond, I am able to focus on the good I did and see how much I have learned and grown along the way.

When I work with clients, I ask them the following questions to guide them through the process of reframing their own mindset:

1. What are the consequences of your current way of thinking, feeling, and acting?
2. What are the facts?
3. What assumptions are you making that might not be true?
4. What can you control?
5. What do you really want, consistent with your deepest values and beliefs?
6. What will inspire you to act in new ways?

You can use these same questions to begin telling your new story.

Once you realize you have agency over your mindset and the power to shift limiting beliefs into empowering ones, you have the rocket fuel to arrive at a fulfilled life. You now have the tools to create a future reality that is different from the current life you are living. You have the power to grow, shift, and propel yourself to any destination you have ever imagined.

# Conclusion

THIS BOOK HAS BEEN AN INVITATION FOR YOU TO STOP SIMPLY letting life happen *to* you and to instead create a life that is built *by* you. It's been an invitation to do BusinessOutside—outside in nature, and outside comfort zones and outdated corporate norms. That's where powerful, positive change lives.

In each chapter, I have provided an opportunity to take an action leading toward a more intentional life, a life driven by a growth mindset. My hope is that you will take the principles in this book and apply them to create a life you love.

Now it's time to take those first steps. Start by working outside of the office more often. Challenge the status quo so that you can move faster and be more innovative. Embrace vulnerability and connect deeply with others. Shake the tree of the mundane. Create a new story.

You have the tools you need to identify your personal values and create your personal values statement. Now it's time to use your personal values statement as a compass. As a reminder, I've provided a Personal Values worksheet along with a Make it Happen worksheet in the Appendix. You can use these to quickly identify your top values, your Zone of Genius, your rockets and anchors, and more. These worksheets allow you to take the first steps into your future. Lean into and harness what you're great at and what you love and try to do those things 90 percent of the time, and then delegate or delete the rest. Choose a one-year personal goal, and then reverse engineer what you will need to do to get there. Reflect on how you are spending your time and energy and make one small change this week to move toward the life you want.

Finally, remember the trail as a metaphor for life. There is always more to achieve. There are always new paths to explore. Rather than compare your journey to anyone else's, be intentional about your own. By doing so, you'll be able to enjoy the journey, not just the destination. On each step of the journey, be sure to return to the primary questions: Who are you? What do you value? What do you want to achieve? Decide which trail to take next and use your compass to keep you headed in the right direction.

# Appendix

# PERSONAL VALUES WORKSHEET

**1)** Look at all the values in the list on the next page and create the importance of each value to you by placing a check in either of these columns:

-Not Important;
-Slightly Important; or
-Really Important

**2)** Look through the values you have marked as really important and choose the ten most important values and checkmark them in the TOP 10 column. If you feel there are any important values missing, write them in the spaces at the bottom.

**3)** Look at your Top 10 Column and choose the five most important values. Check them in the TOP 5 Column. Check them in the TOP 3 Column. These are your core values.

_____ , _____ , _____

**4)** Finally, from your three core values, choose your NUMBER 1, most important value.

_____

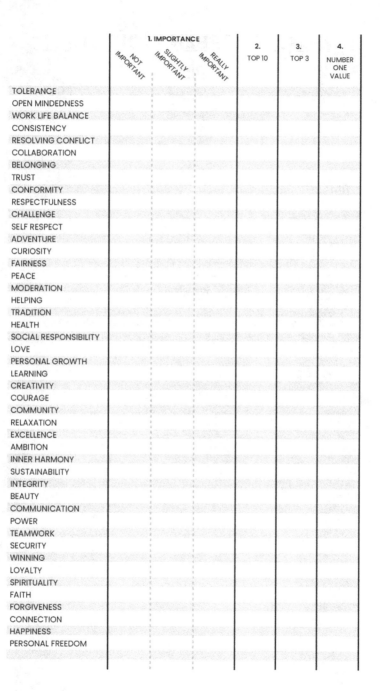

| | 1. IMPORTANCE | | | 2. | 3. | 4. |
|---|---|---|---|---|---|---|
| | NOT IMPORTANT | SLIGHTLY IMPORTANT | REALLY IMPORTANT | TOP 10 | TOP 3 | NUMBER ONE VALUE |
| TOLERANCE | | | | | | |
| OPEN MINDEDNESS | | | | | | |
| WORK LIFE BALANCE | | | | | | |
| CONSISTENCY | | | | | | |
| RESOLVING CONFLICT | | | | | | |
| COLLABORATION | | | | | | |
| BELONGING | | | | | | |
| TRUST | | | | | | |
| CONFORMITY | | | | | | |
| RESPECTFULNESS | | | | | | |
| CHALLENGE | | | | | | |
| SELF RESPECT | | | | | | |
| ADVENTURE | | | | | | |
| CURIOSITY | | | | | | |
| FAIRNESS | | | | | | |
| PEACE | | | | | | |
| MODERATION | | | | | | |
| HELPING | | | | | | |
| TRADITION | | | | | | |
| HEALTH | | | | | | |
| SOCIAL RESPONSIBILITY | | | | | | |
| LOVE | | | | | | |
| PERSONAL GROWTH | | | | | | |
| LEARNING | | | | | | |
| CREATIVITY | | | | | | |
| COURAGE | | | | | | |
| COMMUNITY | | | | | | |
| RELAXATION | | | | | | |
| EXCELLENCE | | | | | | |
| AMBITION | | | | | | |
| INNER HARMONY | | | | | | |
| SUSTAINABILITY | | | | | | |
| INTEGRITY | | | | | | |
| BEAUTY | | | | | | |
| COMMUNICATION | | | | | | |
| POWER | | | | | | |
| TEAMWORK | | | | | | |
| SECURITY | | | | | | |
| WINNING | | | | | | |
| LOYALTY | | | | | | |
| SPIRITUALITY | | | | | | |
| FAITH | | | | | | |
| FORGIVENESS | | | | | | |
| CONNECTION | | | | | | |
| HAPPINESS | | | | | | |
| PERSONAL FREEDOM | | | | | | |

# MAKE IT HAPPEN WORKSHEET

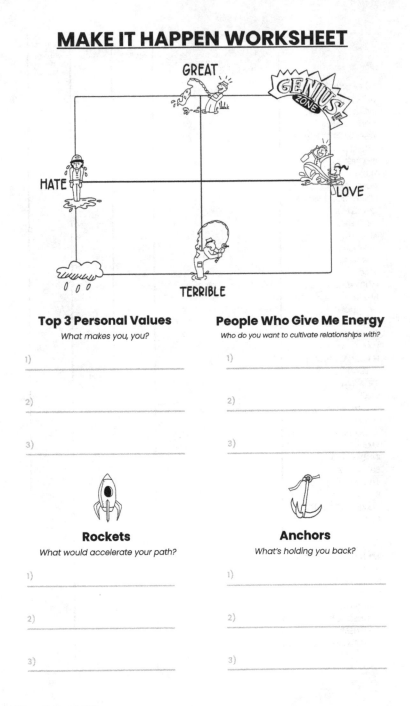

### Top 3 Personal Values
*What makes you, you?*

1) _____

2) _____

3) _____

### People Who Give Me Energy
*Who do you want to cultivate relationships with?*

1) _____

2) _____

3) _____

### Rockets
*What would accelerate your path?*

1) _____

2) _____

3) _____

### Anchors
*What's holding you back?*

1) _____

2) _____

3) _____

## My One-Year Goals

*What one big thing do you want to achieve within 12 months?*

Family: _____

Personal: _____

Business: _____

## My New Experience

*What's one thing you intend to do that is uncomfortable or new within 12 months?*

_____

## Three Things I Can Do to Manage My Energy Better

1) _____

2) _____

3) _____

## Where Do I Want to Spend My Time?

*Create your own pie chart below*

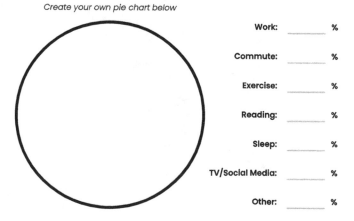

Work: _____ %

Commute: _____ %

Exercise: _____ %

Reading: _____ %

Sleep: _____ %

TV/Social Media: _____ %

Other: _____ %

# Acknowledgments

FIRST AND FOREMOST, I WANT TO THANK MY FAMILY. TO MY WIFE, Aly, whose boundless love and unwavering support grounds me and makes me better; and to our kids, Ansley Kate and Owen—you tolerate my passions with a smile and support my countless endeavors with patience.

To my mom, who always taught me to be strong and believe in myself. To my dad, who taught me the value of relationships and encouraged me to dream big. To my sister, Terri, who taught me the importance of creativity and doing a little bit extra to get noticed. To my brother, Brent, who provided tough love and guidance. And to Tom and Pam for raising the most amazing daughter I could ever imagine, and welcoming me into their family with unconditional love.

I want to acknowledge my YPO Forum mates and personal board of directors: Rob Israel, Christy Orris, Andrew Larson, Anthony Pigliacampo, Bing Howenstein, Linc Turner, and Hansen Rada. Thank you for providing inspiration and guidance in all aspects of my life.

Thank you to the many friends I do BusinessOutside with, for giving me energy, joy, and inspiration, including: Steve Neville, Jason Flynn, Chris Schwallbach, Aaron Houghton, Jon Teaford, Tom Bates, Scott McClelland, Andrew Knowles, Tony Martin, Robby Larkin, Steve Mills, KC Timmons, Rhett Bennett, Jack Swift, Tom Romine, Dave Bacon, Jay Hirsh, Jeremy Wing, Andrew Hyde, Brandon Kuhl, Ret Taylor, David Barlow, Rob Mossman, Dan Mack, Brian Natwick, Brad Jackson, Loren Bendele, Rick Weiner, Jeff Donaldson, Godard Abel, Jim Franklin, Brian McGrath Davis, Regan Ebert, Brian Ciciora, and Lauren Ivison.

To the many clients and friends who encouraged me to write this book, including Carla Mack, Raanan Naftalovich, Carla Piñeyro-Sublett, Dave Brown, Kevin Yapp, Jim Magrann, John Ryan, Susy Yu, Al Ulsifer, Angel Alvarez, Brent Rasmussen, Jean Carrier, Michael Burnette, Tonya Hinch, Derek Dodge, Grady Lenski, John Agwunobi, Tom O'Neil, John Marvin, Jason Bolt, Andy Pawson, Julie Collins, Tony Sommer, and Justin Manning.

To Scott Meece and Tariq Aziz for encouraging me to follow my passion and never give up.

Gratitude to Florence Williams for writing *The Nature Fix*, and inspiring others to get outside. To Harvey Mackay who taught me to *dig my well before I was thirsty.*

To my first YPO Forum mates in Atlanta who encouraged me to live my best life, and realize my full potential: David Cummings, Carl Streck, Andrew Stith, Frank Peeples, Ritt Carrano, Dan Kaufman, Daniel Hathaway.

To Reade Fahs who encouraged me to join YPO and helped

me get my foot in the door at Walmart.

To my colleagues at Sanitas Advisors including John Walborn, Jeff Poe, Jamie Rosin, Matt Oerding, Jamie Gardner, Lita Currie, Jackson Klein, and Riley Ferrero for their continued support. To advisors David Barry, Amy Sorrells, and Marc Hodulich for their sage wisdom and advice.

To contributors, Erin Pheil for helping me get unstuck, and Erin Carson for inspiring me to be better. Thank you to Jared Hanley and his team at NatureFix for leading from the front.

To Lundy Fields and Karen Gough who taught me to "Make it Happen!"

To Linda Anderson, my high school guidance counselor, who helped me realize I was never going to be a doctor. To Miles Hilton-Barber and Walter Leicher who encouraged me to expand my circle of comfort.

To the first employees at SoloHealth, including Stephen Kendig, Eric Hoell, Chad Terry, and Robert Lort, for their tireless efforts and long-standing conviction. And to all the early investors for believing in me, including Tom Lamb, who was my first "boat tapper," guiding and mentoring me to be a better leader.

To the wishing tree on Mt. Sanitas and all the people who I have ever hiked that mountain with who shared their stories and inspired me. To Cesar Kuriyama for creating 1 Second Everyday, allowing me to capture the memorable moments of my life.

To the team who made this book happen including Karen Rowe who did a lot of the heavy lifting, John Mannion for his endless editing and revision, Mikey Kershisnik for keeping the train on the tracks and on time, and to Katherine Shady who brought the cover to life. And a special thanks to the incredibly talented Taryl Hanson for the drawings in this book.

To Jim Sharpe for teaching Aly and me the "zip code strategy," which inspired our move to Boulder. To Jesse Itzler for introducing me to "Building Your Life Resume" and doing more of the things you love to do with the people you love to do them with. And to Joey T for helping me get out of my comfort zone and find adventure in the mountains of Colorado.

Finally, I am so fortunate to have a wonderful group of friends, who through thick and thin have shown love, respect, and loyalty. Thanks to all. Let's Make it Happen!

# About the Author

BART FOSTER IS A FOUNDER, STRATEGIST, ADVISOR, AND COACH to Fortune 500 companies, YPO & Entrepreneurs' Organization (EO) members, and emerging startups. As the founder and managing director of BusinessOutside®, a training and facilitation firm for the future of work, he partners with companies striving to create elite teams and reenergize corporate cultures. BusinessOutside creates unique and customized retreats and curriculums for corporate executives, families, CEO forums, boards of directors, and more.

Bart has experience leading public and private companies in the US and Europe, both as an entrepreneur and intrapreneur, with a focus on innovation at the intersection of consumer, technology, and retail. He works to bridge the gap between large multinational companies that want to be more innovative, and early-stage ventures that need the resources, capital, and expertise of the large corporations.

While working at Novartis, Bart was recognized as the Entrepreneur of the Year for developing a new business venture, which became SoloHealth (now Pursuant Health), a healthcare services company that places self-service kiosks in high traffic retail environments.

Prior to working at Novartis, Bart was a Director for Peachtree Network, a successful Internet start-up based in Montreal, Canada. While there, the company had an IPO on the Canadian Venture Exchange. He began his career with Kellogg's in consumer marketing and sales and was the youngest person to ever win the Golden K Award, salesperson of the year in his second year.

He is a father, husband, IRONMAN Triathlete, Florida Gator, and active in Young President Organization (YPO). He and his wife, Aly, and their two kids enjoy all things outdoors: hiking, fishing, cycling, backcountry skiing, open water swimming. He leads groups and tries to incorporate nature in everything he does. He thrives on thinking differently and helping people realize what is possible.

CPSIA information can be obtained
at www.ICGtesting.com
Printed in the USA
BVHW072110310722
643480BV00001B/53

9 781544 530758